BORDERLINE
41-42
117-130

EXISTENTIAL ART THERAPY
The Canvas Mirror

ABOUT THE AUTHOR

Bruce L. Moon is Director of the Clinical Internship in Art Therapy at the Harding Hospital in Worthington, Ohio. He is also the Chief of Adjunctive Therapy for the Child and Adolescent Division of Harding Hospital and is an instructor in art therapy at the Columbus College of Art and Design. A past president of the Buckeye Art Therapy Association and active committee member at the national level, he has presented papers and workshops throughout the country.

Bruce brings to the profession a rich tradition of combined training in art education, theology and art therapy. The integration of these with his interest in existentialism provides an intriguing, poetic and theoretical approach to art therapy in a psychiatric setting.

As an artist he is an active painter and poet-songwriter. Recently he and his wife, Cathy, also an art therapist, built their own log home in the country outside of Columbus, Ohio, where they live with their two children, Jesse and Brea.

EXISTENTIAL ART THERAPY
The Canvas Mirror

By

BRUCE L. MOON, M.A.C.E., M. DIV., A.T.R.

With a Foreword by

Don L. Jones, A.T.R, H.L.M

CHARLES C THOMAS • PUBLISHER
Springfield • Illinois • U.S.A.

Published and Distributed Throughout the World by

CHARLES C THOMAS • PUBLISHER
2600 South First Street
Springfield, Illinois 62794-9265

© *1990 by* CHARLES C THOMAS • PUBLISHER

ISBN 0-398-05668-4

Library of Congress Catalog Card Number: 89-20670

With THOMAS BOOKS *careful attention is given to all details of manufacturing
and design. It is the Publisher's desire to present books that are satisfactory as to their
physical qualities and artistic possibilities and appropriate for their particular use.*
THOMAS BOOKS *will be true to those laws of quality that assure a good name
and good will.*

Printed in the United States of America
SC-R-3

Library of Congress Cataloging-in-Publication Data

Moon, Bruce L.
    Existential art therapy : the canvas mirror / by Bruce L. Moon ;
with a foreword by Don L. Jones.
        p.   cm.
    Includes bibliographical references (p.   ).
    ISBN 0-398-05668-4
    1. Art therapy.   2. Existential psychotherapy.   I. Title.
RC489.A7M66   1990
615.8′5156 — dc20   89-20670
                                                                          CIP

FOREWORD

Bruce Moon has written more than a textbook. What he gives us is more like a medieval illuminated map, usable for navigation, but populated by dragons. In my view he translates the first of Buddha's four Noble Truths, "Suffering is universal" into "Life is permanent white water" and invites the reader to plunge in.

It is made clear in this work that the existential process of art therapy, though often unpredictable, is not a wild turbulence. There is a history, a sequence: exposure—premise—practice—theory. Bruce builds on the foundations of art therapy that have evolved over the past half-century. The establishment of the Clinical Internship in Art Therapy at Harding Hospital has been an innovative, unique contribution to the field of art therapy education.

There is support from Freud and precedent for promoting arts as a primary mode of treatment. He emphasized the importance of unconscious imagery. If dreams provided the "royal road to be traveled by night from the unconscious," then graphic metaphors might well be expressways to convey feelings when ordinary routes are impassable. Jung suggested, "There must not only be talk, but doing something about it." Years of art therapy practice have confirmed that affects can surface directly into consciousness without traveling the circuitous route of word associations.

The process Freud labeled "hypercathexis"—which included an enabling space, acute focus of attention, guided imagery, a relationship and sensitive coaching—is a supportive treatment context for the art therapist as well as the patient. It is the raft on the white water.

Some who read this book may conclude that the man is the message, implying that events portrayed in the case studies are personality centered and therefore unteachable. There is truth in the cliche, but both the man and the message are also a blend of history, talent, training, experience and team practice. Glimpses of creative practitioners at work in the mainstream are vital for students, colleagues of other disciplines and others who strive to understand the classical tutorial methods that are the model for clinical training in art therapy.

Bruce has taken personal risks in sharing revealing encounters with patients and with himself. One hopes he is appreciated for having highlighted the importance of existential aspects of art therapy in treatment and training.

Don L. Jones, A.T.R., H.L.M.

PREFACE

By means of image and parable one can persuade, but can prove nothing. That is why the world of science and learning is so wary of image and parable.

Frederick Neitsche

The title of this book is an expression of my desire to link the practice of art psychotherapy to the core issues of life as presented in existentialism. In this decade the health care systems in America seem to have drifted away from focus on quality of life and relationships towards preoccupation with observable, quantifiable and verifiable data regarding functional behaviors of the patient. They have exchanged the language of psychotherapy—a journey into the deep inner self—for a more pragmatic and cost-efficient language of DRG, DSM–III–R and empirical evidence. In so doing they have banished from discussion much of the wisdom of centuries of our collective struggle to understand ourselves, what we mean to one another and our place in the universe. The poetry of clinical communication has been discolored, disinfected and at times altogether removed.

Art psychotherapy has not been immune to this trend. At conferences and symposia I find myself wondering what happened to the depth and richness of my field. This may explain my need to write at this time. My colleague and friend, John Reece, says I have written it "to find a stage large enough for my ego." Perhaps.

Existentialism implies an interest in the human struggle with deep issues of life in the face of death. Anxiety, conscience, relationships, concern, guilt and love all receive significant attention from prominent existential writers. Existentialists often choose to present their thoughts through story and metaphor rather than the classic dialogue form of Plato. They seem less interested in intellectual discourse than in wholistic, provocative imagining. In linking art psychotherapy to existentialism I make no claim to represent the perspective of all art psychotherapists. The reader who seeks formulas for interpretation or outlines of specific technical exercises will be disappointed. There are occasional references to experiences or structures, but these are tucked safely in the deeper discussion of illustrative cases. I have no desire to write a clinical cookbook; rather, I intend to frame a manner of thinking about what I do as an art psychotherapist. My colleagues in the *quality assurance* field will no doubt find this work inefficient and vague, even non-intentional. So be it.

I consider all intentionally helping professions to be forms of art. Therefore, all therapists are essentially artists. In spite of the increasing interest, research and speculation about the biological and chemical roots of behavior and personality, the process of treating the patient continues to be more akin to art than science. In my experience as a clinician I have used a variety of action-oriented treatment techniques. I have engaged with patients in music, sports, poetry and work, but it is in the visual image that I am most at home. The consistent theme of my writings and teachings over the past fifteen years has been an insistence on honoring the graphic metaphors of my patients. I am perturbed that some of my colleagues in art therapy and related disciplines appear to have lost their identity as artists. Their vision of creativity, growth and meaning has been traded in for a perception of self as scientist or modifier of behavior. This book is about the depths of our profession as I see it, integral to the depths of art and artists and of human existence.

A foremost art historian, H. W. Janson, uses the metaphor of birth to describe the process of creating art. I like this metaphor and wish I had thought of it first. I will refer to it often. Birth is a basic life event. It involves an initial act of love followed by patience, preparation and surprise. My wife Cathy assures me that labor is an apt description of the process, "It's awfully hard work." I can attest to the intensity that birthing involves, having been an eye witness and coach on two occasions. Art psychotherapy as a discipline is still being born.

This book is about the life of our field. Just as when my children were born I could only try to imagine what they might grow into, so we can only glimpse the future of our profession. As children grow they gradually master tasks and form their identity. We cheer their successes, encourage their struggles and applaud their accomplishments. Sometimes they make mistakes and take a wrong direction. In those times we redirect, challenge and point out other roads to travel. As a participant in the birthing of art psychotherapy I look with loving, critical and hopeful eyes at our discipline. There are questions to be raised, directions to be challenged and praises to be sung.

The Canvas Mirror, subtitle of this book, is poetic self-indulgence. Over the past twenty years I have often experienced my paintings as a great comfort in the midst of anxiety or pain. Sometimes, feeling comfortable and self-satisfied, I have been jabbed and torn by my own art. That is the intent of this book. It is what I am committed to. As you read on, may you share both the soothing and the affliction I have felt. May we all connect with the joy, pain and *awfully hard work* of being born.

If a man loses anything and goes back and looks carefully for it, he will find it.
Tatanka Yotanka (Sitting Bull)

Bruce L. Moon

AUTHOR'S NOTE

The clinical accounts in this book are in spirit true. In all instances, however, names have been changed and biographical information about patients has been so obscured as to totally insure the privacy and confidentiality of the persons with whom I have worked.

In some instances the illustrations are amalgamations of many specific cases, again with factual data fictionalized to protect individual identities.

The drawings and paintings discussed in case illustrations are based on patient work. The original works are the property of the individuals who made them. The descriptions have been sufficiently altered as to guard the integrity and privacy of their creators. In no case have I used the actual art product of my patient. I believe that to do so would not add significantly to the content or intent of this book.

ACKNOWLEDGMENTS

I am indebted to many people who have, in their ways, contributed to the writing of this book. Special thanks go to Ellie Jones, my editor and colleague. She took a rough stone and polished it beautifully. Thanks to those who read, criticized and encouraged along the way—Cathy Moon, Deb DeBrular, John Reece and others. Thanks to Don Jones, my mentor, who believed in me in those times of my greatest doubts.

I've been blessed, these past fifteen years, to work with a creative, conflictual, painful and fun staff of the Adjunctive Therapy Department. In many ways this book is about the lessons they've taught me. I thank the administration of the Harding Hospital who supported this effort with time, encouragement and considerable typing and retyping hours. Doctor Richard Griffin, past Medical Director, offered help in a variety of ways from the earliest stages of the work.

Finally, I want to thank the patients I've come to know over the years. It is they who've taught me most of what I know. It is their stories, their anguish that bonded together art psychotherapy and existentialism so tightly within me.

To all these . . . thank you!

B.L.M.

CONTENTS

EXISTENTIAL ART THERAPY
The Canvas Mirror

Chapter I

PERSPECTIVE: WHERE IT BEGINS...

Some time ago I was in the art studio at Harding Hospital in Worthington, Ohio. I was working with an adolescent girl on the fundamentals of drawing one- and two-point perspective. She just wasn't getting it and I was frustrated with her seeming inability to grasp the concept of vanishing points. She would ask questions like "Are they real?" and "Who put them there?" The more she questioned, the more exasperated I became. Finally I suggested we take a break from this formal process and that she just sketch for a while. I moved to an adjoining room to work on a painting I had in progress.

After a few minutes, the girl entered the painting studio looking relaxed and pleased with herself. She held up a piece of drawing paper on which were several small drawings of cubes, utilizing one- and two-point perspective techniques. I smiled and asked how she'd figured it out. She laughed and told me that I'd been presenting things all wrong. She said, "They aren't *vanishing* points, they are *beginning* points, and I can put them wherever I want." I may never again be comfortable in referring to those imaginary points as vanishing points. They will always be beginning points.

The notion that the beginnings of things are on the distant horizon appeals to me. It implies a close relationship of foreground to background and of object to environment. This view holds a sense of breadth and depth which shifts focus away from the specific object right in front of our faces and connects us with a much wider spectrum of possibilities. When we add to this the proposition that beginning points are wherever we want them to be, we immediately sense the paradoxical nature of our work. As we think of art and treatment, growth and expression, the polarities are endless. A few examples are the continuums of temporal to infinite, specific to universal, shallows to depths, profane to sacred, and so on.

Where to begin this exploration of existential art psychotherapy? The possible points of departure are many. For instance, I could start with the

primitive cave paintings in France, or Michelangelo's idea of freeing
the form from the marble block, or from the confessional cell of
Catholicism, or the library of Sigmund Freud, or the writing desk of
Jean Paul Sartre, or . . . , or . . . , or . . .

In the song "Crossroads,"[1] the poet-songwriter Don McLean offers
useful reflections about beginnings. Listen:

> *You know I've heard about people like me*
> *but I never made the connection*
> *they walk one road to set them free*
> *and find they've gone the wrong direction*
> *But there's no need for turning back*
> *'cause all roads lead to where I stand*
> *and I believe I'll walk them all*
> *no matter what I may have planned.*

Regardless of where I start, all roads will take me to where I am. Let's
go for a walk.

Chapter II

EXISTENTIAL VALUES/ARTISTIC TRADITIONS

Existentialism has often been misinterpreted as a philosophy of despair. Readers of existentialistic literature occasionally find themselves so burdened by the existentialist's rejection of traditional values that they fail to hear the subtle, yet constant undertone of hope. It is easy to hear the themes of doubt. The existentialists' skepticism that humanity can find self-fulfilment through wealth, fame or pleasure is often perceived as cold, bitter and impersonal. Their recognition that all life is marked by suffering and loss mocks the ordinary person's attempt at achieving somehow a full and happy life. The existentialist position that pain, frustration, guilt and anxiety are the unavoidable lot of human beings is disquieting to say the least, particularly in this era which so adores the material manifestations of success and achievement.

Those who see the existentialist's embrace of these life realities too often fail to see the accompanying belief that painful striving is what generates values that go beyond the materialistic—the only values, in the end, that may genuinely be realized and felt to be truly worthy of human searching.

The existentialist literature is unpopular with many because of its insistence that humankind's struggle for worldly goods is a misperception of the human condition, that it leads people to petty, shallow lives and away from what could be a noble struggle. At the same time, the existential rejection of the *ivory tower* detachment of traditional philosophers is based on the belief that such distant objectivity impoverishes the human spirit by causing it to lose its uniquely human dimensions. So it is that the existentialists declare their values to be distinct from those of ordinary materialists and hedonists and distinct from those of traditional philosophers. Existentialism charges both with inhumanity, since the underlying motivation of both is the desire for a condition of well-being that is impossible and devalues humans.

One difficulty many readers have with existential literature is that authors are not always in agreement with one another. There are, however, some basic common themes that consistently appear.

There is a clear acceptance of the belief that suffering, anguish and struggle are essential elements of life and are universally experienced. One may paint a pretty picture or render a subject skillfully without having known suffering, but the existentialists would insist that this will never be considered a great painting. Rather, it is a clever illustration. Similarly, persons may say that they love each another, but if they have not weathered pain, their love can be nothing more than a sugar glaze, since for the existentialist love grows from the awareness that death or abandonment is always possible. Love is an attitude of concern based upon the potential for irreparable suffering.

The existentialist is dedicated to freeing humanity from its denial of inescapable anxieties, fears and shallow routines.

Finally, existential values focus the awareness and call for passionate and active engagement with life as it is.

In summary, existentialists' values grow out of an intense consciousness of the tragic and noble potential of the human situation. They are dedicated to liberating the individual from fears and anxieties and they are known for their intense experience of life. For the existentialist the primary value of life is to live it to the fullest, as demonstrated in actions of free choice, assertion, love and creative work. Accordingly, these manifestations of intensity are not possible without pain, struggle and risk.

Central to understanding my interest in existentialism as an essential element of art psychotherapy is the existentialist's analysis of the human condition. Crucial to this is the experience of anguish. In existential thought, anguish is conceived as an extremely intense experience, linked with distinct affective tones. At one extreme are terror and dread; at the other, awe and exhilaration. At times these emotional opposites swirl together. In other circumstances they succeed one another. The existentialist believes that both emotional poles must be present, regardless of order. Existential anguish is most often associated with individual experiences of nothingness, randomness and freedom.

It is the anguish of life that has so often been the dwelling place of the artist. It is certainly the figurative home of many severely disturbed psychiatric patients that I have known over the years. I have watched as a young woman, after having completed a drawing of her "prison," turned and began to smash the windows of the studio, raking her arms across the pieces of glass. I have carried her bloodstains on my hands for years. In those days I misperceived my mission as therapist. I thought my task was to make her feel better. If that woman were my patient today, I would make no attempt to lighten her burden or ease her suffering. I would instead pay homage to her pain. I would be with her in the midst of her anguish and I would honor my own suffering.

Artist therapists are in a unique position to treat the existential concerns of the emotionally disturbed patient. Throughout all history the poet, the playwright and the painter have abandoned the pursuits of pleasure, wealth and fame in search of values that go deeper than hedonistic materialism. As artists we have a long tradition of being seekers of meaning in life. We have always been willing to suffer in our quest. We have always volunteered ourselves during the journey and we are well acquainted with the dualisms of anguish. It is this artistic tradition of courage that can be our special gift to our patients.

Whenever I meet a new patient I remind myself that I am in the company of not only a diagnosed cluster of symptoms; I remind myself that I am in the company of not only a manifestation of developmental theories; I remind myself that I am in the company of not only behavioral patterns and pathology . . . I remind myself that I am in the company of a fellow human being whose life has a meaning all its own.

I am not a scientist or a researcher. I am an artist, a husband and a father. I look at the world through an existentialist's eyes. My life's work is art psychotherapy.

Let me share it with you.

Chapter III

METAPHOR, RITUAL AND JOURNEY

A story. . . .

Some time ago, in a primitive land, the natives of a certain village awoke to find that during the night a large silver bird had come to rest in their clearing. The chief of the tribe sent word to all the huts and soon after sunrise all the folk of the village stood at the edge of their clearing, watching what they presumed was God sleeping. When the pilot roused from his sleep, he was taken aback as he peered out the cockpit window to see row upon row of men, women and children staring silently at his plane.

Cautiously he opened the side hatch and walked out on a wing. The tribe fell to the ground as one, quivering and praying that they would not be harmed by the golden-haired man who sprang from the side of God. The pilot began to laugh. He was, after all, a modern educated man and an atheist at that. *Such foolishness,* he thought. *I will teach these primitive fools all about airplanes,* he decided. He raised his hands and beckoned the people forward. Gradually the simple folk arose and approached. When all had come closer, the pilot turned grandly and re-entered his craft. He engaged the engines. With a dramatic roar, the propellors spun. Lights flashed.

He looked out the window again and was irritated to see all the natives lying face down in the dirt as before. He turned off the engines and went back out on the wing, trying desperately to think of some way to teach these backward people. He began to speak. At a silent signal from the chief, all the men raised their spears and threw. The pilot died instantly.

The natives erected a shrine on the spot. Each year they offer sacrifice in hopes that God will never roar at them again. So far it is working.

The modern, well-educated pilot had failed to realize the awesome power of the metaphor that he was. People are not automatically freed by facts. Sadly, truth does not change attitudes, beliefs or biases. Some define the purpose of therapy to be helping individuals to know and accept the truth about themselves. Of course, the difficulty for therapists is distinguishing *whose* truth they are dealing with—their own or their patients'.

In any case, the telling of truths by therapists is always a risky business, for it may rob the patients of their opportunity for growth. It may also steal from them a sense of responsibility, whether for success or failure. This is not to say that patients, at times, don't enjoy this theft. Many times the patient demands of the therapist, "Tell me what I have to do!"

Geometrists tell us that the shortest distance between any two points is a straight line. This truth should not be applied to psychotherapy, however. If entry into treatment is symbolized by one point and termination of therapy by another, the course between is seldom straight. More often it is comprised of unexpected curves, deadend spirals, avenues that go nowhere and treacherous paths on which there is no easy way to tread. The metaphor I use most often to describe art psychotherapy is a journey or pilgrimage.

In his work *The Arts and Psychotherapy*,[2] Shawn McNiff has eloquently offered the image of the art therapist as *shaman*. The shaman starts his special life by going on his own painful journey. Along his tortured path he gradually masters his turmoil by facing monsters, demons and malevolent forces. A partnership is struck between the shaman's heroic virtues and these evil potentials as he experiences the battle within his own soul. Thus the shaman learns to live with the motives, forces and conflicts that most people in his world attempt to devalue and disown. The power of his healing is formed in his willingness to go with those who come to him for help as they make their own internal pilgrimage. In this way the shaman embodies valuing and ownership of the difficult, potent inner world of those who seek his wisdom.

Essential to the healing power of the shaman and the art therapist is the use of metaphor. Seldom speaking his truth bluntly, the shaman pushes the seeker to explore his own mysteries and decide for himself the meaning of the journey. So, too, the art therapist, using graphic metaphor, challenges the patient to discover the meaning of the psychotherapy journey. The shaman and the art therapist know full well that the seeker/patient already has the power to heal himself, but lacks faith in that capacity. The metaphors guide the seeker to explore himself, to use his imagination and create his own solutions to give his life meaning.

In literature, a metaphor is a device in which one thing is described in the terms of another. The combining of these images sheds new light on the character being described. For instance, in the classic story *The Wizard of Oz,* Dorothy's journey down the yellow brick road to Oz can be viewed as a metaphor of each human being's quest for what is of genuine value in life. The Scarecrow, Tin Man and Lion are symbols of heroism and goodness within the search. The witches, hostile forest and flying monkeys represent obstacles and the villain that lurks inside each of us.

Theologians discuss metaphor as a concept that holds in tension the potential for multiple interpretations; their purpose being to illuminate or expose truth. An example is the story of Jesus walking across the water to his frightened disciples' boat during a storm. One interpreter refers to the miracle in the story and focuses on the wondrous nature of God to his followers. Another reader of the same passage may be reassured by considering it to be a factual recounting of a marvelous historical event. Still another may approach the passage from a more poetic perspective and liken the person of Jesus to anyone who is able to transcend the turmoil of life's storms and chaos. From each viewpoint there is truth expressed regarding the nature of faith.

My students, at both the Columbus College of Art and Design and Harding Hospital, often question the use of metaphor in therapy. "Why beat around the bush?" they ask. I respond.

In "Hearts and Bones," Paul Simon sings:

> *and after awhile they fell apart*
> *it wasn't hard to do*
> *everybody loves the sound of a train*
> *in the distance*
> *everybody thinks it's true*[3]

It would have been much more direct and to the point if Paul had written, "We don't love each other anymore," but the power and beauty, the wistful loneliness of the communication would have been lost. As I listen to him sing I feel the rhythm of the train. I hear its whistle and experience again the feelings I had when some of my own past relationships deteriorated. The metaphor of a train in the distance allows me to participate. It is not just Paul Simon singing about himself. He sings about me.

My students sometimes smile and nod their understanding. At other times they look at me bewildered, as if to say, *Bruce, you haven't understood our question. Why beat around the bush?*

When my daughter, Brea, was very small, we worried a lot about her being near the wood stove and fireplace tools. One day she grabbed the poker just after it had been pulled from the fire. It was a very painful learning experience for her, but we've not had to warn her since. This illustrates something very basic about most of us. We want to discover truth, not have it told to us by another. In his book, *If You Meet the Buddha on the Road, Kill Him,*[4] Doctor Sheldon Kopp observes, "The most important things each man must learn for himself." The patients I treat in the clinical setting come bearing their emotional burns and scars which, for one reason or another, they have been unable to learn from. The last thing they need from me is a lecture on why or how they've managed to be burned so often, so severely. Rather, I attempt to engage them in the metaphor of journey.

Art psychotherapists are by nature metaphoreticians. It is our role to see, listen and interact with the symbolic graphic language and actions of our patients. Beyond this, it seems imperative to me that we not only act as receptors of patient-generated communications but in turn respond through metaphor. Perhaps if the aforementioned pilot had understood the power of the metaphor he was a part of and had been able to respond appropriately within the metaphor, he might have lived to tell about it.

Again, metaphor is defined as a manner of speaking. I propose that we go beyond the verbal denotations of this definition. We must deepen and expand our thinking about what metaphors are. I have reservations about the need we therapists often seem to have to talk. We want to be sure that the patient is getting the point of what he is experiencing. When we can move beyond the notion of *verbal* metaphor and conceptualize *visual* and *action* metaphors, we begin to glimpse the depth inherent in our field and our own potential as healers.

To translate the myth/metaphor into symbol and action within the psychotherapy milieu is to do what rituals have done within religious communities for centuries. The ritual of the eucharist, for instance, is the story/metaphor expressed through the symbolic actions of breaking bread and drinking wine. Here again, the metaphor lends itself to multiple interpretations and understandings of the actions, ranging from re-enactment of an actual event, to recapitulation of a miraculous transubstantiation, to dramatization of existential poetry regarding human brokenness.

The rituals I engage in as an art psychotherapist are the doings of art. The gathering of materials and preparation of the studio are the beginning steps of the ritual dance that moves from soul to brush to canvas. The metaphors in which I move are often not thought out beforehand.

They emerge as the dance proceeds. This ritual doing of art is always an intense inward journey. As one of my patients recently described it, "It's like I'm standing on the edge of a cliff and I can't tell if it's swirling water below or fire. I can't stay where I am. I know I have to step over the edge."

I was deeply moved by these words. They seem to capture the essence of the courage that is required to begin the psychotherapy pilgrimage. One senses the urgency, the fear and the pain that this patient experienced as he spoke and that he anticipated in his future.

My response was to look intently at his drawing and say, quietly, "Yes, I know that feeling. That's the way it is when I begin journeys, too." The patient seemed relieved at this, and I suggested that he invite me along as he stepped over the edge. He asked, "Will you make it less painful?"

I said, "No, but I will be there with you."

It is our task in art therapy, along with other action-oriented disciplines, to engage in the rituals of healing with our patients. In the doing of art, work and play we enact the themes of the therapeutic journey. Our primary task is to listen to and tell stories through action. We hardly need to talk at all. Despite the complexities of individual patient histories and pathological dynamics, there are recurring metaphoric themes with hospitalized patients. This first became clear to me as I read Doctor Donald Rinsley's *Treatment of the Severely Disturbed Adolescent.*[5]

Focusing on inpatient treatment of adolescents, Rinsley isolates three basic messages:

> "I am bad."
> "I am about to lose control."
> "I am afraid you will abandon me."

Over the past fifteen years I have witnessed these metaphoric messages being expressed time and again in a host of activity arenas. I have been there as they pour onto the page in splashes of dramatic color. I have watched as they are pounded into wedging clay and I have listened to their dissonant melodies.

The metaphors of adults are generally more subtle. Grown-ups lose the drama of adolescent immediacy. To the therapist, however, the messages of adult patients can present a covert sense of threat and disease. Often less evident in behavioral expression, these themes are more clearly existential and more likely to plague us all at some time in our adult lives. They are:

"I am lost."

"Somewhere somebody knows the answer."

Following are some illustrations of these recurring metaphoric messages acted out in the therapeutic milieu. I caution the reader to keep in mind that I am speaking only from the perspective of the ritual acting out, the dramatization of the metaphor. While the things I will discuss were happening, significant work was also being done by the various other treatment team disciplines, i.e., psychiatry, social work and nursing. Also, for the sake of clarity I will focus on the metaphoric messages individually. I do not mean to imply that these experiences are exclusive. More often they swirl together to form a complex interaction of dynamic intra- and interpersonal affective experience. Please regard the following illustrations as analogous to two-dimensional overlays which, when viewed together, offer a glimpse of the three-dimensional individual patient.

I AM BAD

Julie came into the hospital with a long history of antisocial and self-destructive behavior. She had engaged in vandalism, theft, substance abuse, had been sexually promiscuous and a runaway. My first impression of her was that she was a hardened and street-wise kid. She said she hated her parents and all other adults. Her parents, after years of battling with Julie, had finally lost control of her and for their own protection had withdrawn. Julie's response was to escalate her bad behavior until the courts intervened. She was admitted to the hospital after several terms in a variety of detention centers and short-term psychiatric settings. Despite her tough exterior there was something oddly likeable about Julie. She had a dry sense of humor, and although she had failed repeatedly in school, one sensed a basic intelligence about her.

When she first entered the therapeutic milieu, the team scheduled her into a *gratifying* regimen. It was their hope that Julie could engage in activities that would foster her strengths and allow her to form relationships based on her positive attributes. Initially, her program included ceramics, music and drama. After four or five weeks it became evident that this plan was having no impact. In ceramics Julie ignored the instructions of the therapist, took shortcuts and refused to wedge her clay properly. This resulted in her pieces exploding in the kiln, ruining her own and others' work.

In music, she was uninterested in learning where to place her fingers on the neck of the guitar. Rather, she spent the session posing with the instrument, imagining herself on an album cover, with no thought of the hours of disciplined practice it would require to learn her first song. In drama she consistently designed roles of bitchy women who intimidated others. Her peers grew to detest her involvement.

It was clear that the treatment team had erred in attempting to provide gratifying experiences. Since Julie's underlying self-view was that she was bad, she interpreted all efforts to enhance her self-esteem as staff stupidity. Her message was, *Since I am a bad person, you are foolish to try to make me like myself. Your foolishness makes you worthless to me.*

The team decided to take another approach. Julie was withdrawn from ceramics, music and drama, and scheduled into wedging, gardening and expressive art. It happened that I was assigned to be her therapist in both the expressive art group and gardening. While her drawings in the group were interesting and her style of engagement intense, it was our work together in the garden that best illustrates Julie's metaphoric expression and my metaphoric response.

It was late March when Julie entered the gardening activity. For the first several weeks I assigned her the task of shoveling horse manure and spreading it on the unplowed garden area. I worked alongside her. She was, to put it mildly, vocal in her resistance to the activity and her feelings about me. Her vocabulary was extensive and I was called many things I had never heard before. Regardless of how crude were her descriptions of me, I consistently worked beside her, ankle deep in manure, and I was always there the next day ready to wade in with her again.

After a couple of weeks of the two of us shoveling together, she stopped one afternoon, leaned on her shovel and asked, "Why in hell do the other kids get to sit on their asses in the greenhouse and play with plants and all I ever get to do is shovel shit?"

I kept working and responded matter-of-factly, "Because this is where you are, Julie." That seemed to make sense to her and she returned to the task.

When the fertilizing was completed, we moved on to other equally non-gratifying tasks: weeding flower beds, making tomato stakes and digging postholes. Other patients in the group planted seeds, watered plants and trimmed flowers. Julie and I talked very little, but I always worked side by side with her in whatever task she was assigned. One afternoon in May, as we pushed our wheelbarrows full of mulch, Julie sighed, "I wish my dad was like you."

"Why's that?" I asked.

"I don't know, I guess you're safe."

When I related this exchange to the treatment team, her psychiatrist exclaimed that it was time to celebrate. He said he believed we had come to the end of Julie's resistance to therapy. He felt she had begun to introspect and was feeling secure enough to share her thoughts with another.

The critical element of this phase of Julie's therapeutic journey was that her metaphorical messages and my responses were almost entirely nonverbal. I let her know that I understood how she felt about herself by providing an environment that matched her self-perception, i.e., horse manure. I saw Julie as she saw herself, and no matter how ugly or tough that could be, regardless of what names she might call me, I was still there the next day, waiting to work with her. My being with her in the midst of her *badness* formed a foundation of emotional support and psychic energy she needed to begin to explore the difficult issues of her therapy.

After nearly a year of intensive work in the hospital, Julie symbolized our relationship in her last drawing in the expressive art psychotherapy group. She drew a pile of horse manure and a long shovel attached to a heart. She said, "When I came here I was hard and weak. Now I'm soft and strong."

I AM ABOUT TO LOSE CONTROL

Steve was a tough kid, angry at the world. He wanted everyone to know it. He gave the nursing staff a horrible time with his aggressive and assaultive behavior. He often disrupted the unit, kicking furniture, hitting walls and slamming doors. Sometimes Steve abruptly walked out of his psychotherapy sessions, screaming obscenities as he stormed down the hall. He was full of rage. In his calmer times, however, he would admit that he was frightened that someday he might do serious harm to himself or someone else. "I don't know why I'm so mad all the time. I hardly ever feel anything else," he lamented.

The story Steve told through his actions was that of a boy starving for relationships. His parents had divorced when he was young, with custody of Steve going to his dad. Mother had dropped out of the picture years ago. Steve's father was a construction worker, task-oriented with few social skills. He had done the best he could, but the job of being a single parent had been too much for him. Steve recalled that his happiest times were when he and his father had built a garage together.

The one place in the hospital environment where Steve was not a behavior problem was the log-sawing activity. Old-style two-man cross-cut saws are used to cut huge old hickory and oak trees culled from the hospital woods. When the sections are cut, they are split into firewood, using sledgehammers, wedges and splitting mauls. This activity is a dramatic enactment of controlled destruction. Although I no longer work in this area, I was a co-therapist in log sawing for eight or nine years. My co-therapist, John McDonough, and I seldom spoke during the sessions. Rather, we used our own engagement in the task to role model struggle, hard work and cooperation.

As Christmas neared, Steve came to a significant period in his thera-peutic journey. He arrived for log sawing just after having been told by the treatment team that he would not be going home for the holidays. As the session progressed, the boy became increasingly agitated. Suddenly, he picked up a maul and began to chop wildly at logs, with no regard for the safety of other people in the area. It was no time for discussion. As he got to the end of one crazy swing, I moved in and forced the maul from his grasp. I wrestled with him back toward the cottage.

As we neared the front door, Steve began to cry. His struggling sub-sided and my controlling grip became caring—holding.

The following day he was quiet and embarrassed. He avoided eye contact with John and me. He appeared to want to apologize for his outburst of the day before, but the words would not come. As everyone else began to work, Steve approached me and asked if we could work together. The log he chose was an oak trunk nearly four feet in diameter. It took us three grueling work sessions to cut through that old tree. As we made the last cut and the trunk cracked and fell apart, Steve's peers cheered. His apology was accepted.

The significant aspects of this process were that we recognized Steve's metaphoric message and provided him with an opportunity to vent his destructive energy in an acceptable manner. We set clear limits on his explosivity, giving him the security of control. Finally, John and I used the action metaphor as a vehicle to relate to Steve on a variety of levels, unlike his family.

In the last two months of Steve's hospitalization, he asked to be in the art studio where I taught painting. There, too, we seldom talked about treatment issues; we did therapy. While he was in the hospital, Steve learned through experience that his rage could be harnessed and that adults could become his allies. By the time he was discharged, he had begun to heal himself.

I AM AFRAID YOU WILL ABANDON ME

While each of the metaphoric messages of adolescence are expressed often, it seems it is this third one I hear the loudest. The very fact of parents leaving their child in the care of the hospital staff is an act of abandonment. A dramatic, traumatic event in the life of an adolescent, it likely symbolizes a long series of more subtle abandonments in the past. Even the life tasks of the adolescent are in one sense an abandonment of childhood and a welcoming of adulthood.

Marie entered the expressive art psychotherapy group after five months of treatment in our hospital and nearly a year of treatment in other settings. Still, she showed little attachment to either her psychotherapist or the unit staff. She was aloof and alone. One way she both maintained her distance and yet demanded interaction was self-mutilation by cutting. Her peers dubbed her "the queen of the cutters" and the insides of her forearms bore gruesome testimony to the accuracy of the title.

For several weeks in the group she would draw but refused to say anything about her images. Rather than confront this behavior, which was atypical in the group, I chose to make a simple comment each time and then go on. I said, "Marie, trust me." Very gradually she began to attach herself to the group by offering observations about others' work. After two or three months of her minimal involvement in the group, I opened a session by telling this story:

"Once there was a man who longed for a pet. He thought about dogs and cats and even little white rats, but none of these seemed to be just what he wanted. One day as he strolled through a park, he saw a small grey rabbit by a bush. *Aha,* he said to himself, *a bunny! That's what I want to be my pet.* So he walked toward the rabbit, but as soon as he got close, the rabbit bounded away. This made the man very sad and he felt even lonelier than before. Then he had an idea. He went to a sporting goods store and bought a fisherman's net. The next day, when he saw the bunny near the bush, he lunged toward it with his new net. The rabbit dodged and ran away. That night, undaunted, he built a trap using a cardboard box, some string and a stick. Early next morning, he set the trap by the bush in the park and placed a carrot under the box as bait. The bunny, however, could smell the scent of the man and would not approach the carrot. The man was quite dejected. The next day he went to the park and sat down on the grass and watched the rabbit. He did that for many days in a row. Each day the bunny would come a little closer to the man. At last, one wonderful day, the rabbit crept close and nuzzled the man's hand."

I asked the group to draw their reactions to this story. Marie drew caricatures of herself and me sitting under a tree. When it came her turn to talk about her drawing, she looked at me and said, "Bruce, I think I trust you."

For the next seven months the expressive art psychotherapy sessions with Marie were somewhat like games of chess. Each of her moves was designed to test my faithfulness; each of mine to counter her suspicions and fears. The essential question for Marie was, *Would I, like so many others in her life, abandon her?*

Several months after her discharge I received a letter from Marie—a poem:

> *Dear Bruce,*
>
> > *This says it all:*
> >
> > *When I left I thought, it's over*
> > *I hurt so much inside*
> > *You said friendship lasts*
> > *I thought you had lied*
> >
> > *But I don't have to be there*
> > *To recall things we said*
> > *Trust me, trust me, trust me*
> > *A good path you always led*
> >
> > *I think I understand it now*
> > *It doesn't matter where*
> > *It's the love and trust inside*
> > *That makes friends be there*
> >
> > *Thanks,*
> >
> > > *Marie*
>
> *Friendship is not bound by space and time.*
> > Richard Bach
> > *Jonathan Livingston Seagull*[6]

I AM LOST

Lenore was an attractive woman, 31 years old, wife, mother of two. Her children were aged 12 and 9. She had married a few weeks after graduating from high school. Her first son was born a little less than one year later. For the first several years of her marriage Lenore and her husband were happy, she said. Then, "I knew deep down inside myself that something was going wrong, but I was too afraid to say anything."

She went on, "When I got pregnant the second time, I was relieved. I remembered how happy we were when my first son was born. I hoped that we could be that happy again. . . . "

Lenore's husband had moved out of their home two months before she was admitted to the hospital. He had moved in with a girlfriend whom he had met at work. Lenore said, "I think it was when my second son was two or three. One morning I woke up and looked over at my husband and realized I didn't know this man. And what was worse, I didn't know who I was." When her husband left her, Lenore quit everything. She quit doing housework, she quit taking care of her sons, she even quit getting out of bed in the morning. She quit.

As I laid out the structure of what I wanted her to do, Lenore looked at me with bewilderment. I had handed her a common cardboard box.

Bruce: I want you to imagine that this box is a symbol of yourself, Lenore. On the outside I want you to paint it or use pictures from magazines to cover it with images about your hobbies or interests—things that any casual acquaintance might know about you.

Lenore: I don't have any.

Bruce: Then, on the inside I want you to think of things that you feel very deeply about, things you believe in or value. Then paint or draw images of those things.

Lenore: I don't have any.

Bruce: What?

Lenore: I don't have any interests or hobbies and I don't believe in anything anymore!

Bruce: Nothing.

Lenore: Nothing.

Bruce: Ah, come on now. Surely there must be something you. . . .

Lenore: I said nothing and I mean nothing. This is a mistake. I shouldn't be here. Call the attendant and get me back to the unit. I'm wasting your time.

Bruce: Hmm. Well, look, you're supposed to be here for an hour. It'll take some time for them to get back here. Why not do something while you wait?

Lenore: This is pointless.

Bruce: I'll call the attendant in a minute. But why don't you go ahead and get started?

Lenore: (sigh) What do you want me to do?

Bruce: Well, you said there is nothing you like to do and you have nothing to believe in. What color would you say *nothing* is?

Lenore: I don't know. . . . white, maybe.

Bruce: Okay, what I want you to do is paint the box white. Inside and out.

When she finished, I commented that I could still see the lettering that had been printed on the outside of the box and that she had not done the bottom of the box.

Lenore: Well, I couldn't do the bottom because everything else was wet.

She sounded angry with me.

Bruce: What do you care? It doesn't mean anything, anyway. Remember, you are painting nothing. And by the way, it needs another coat. It can't be nothing if I can read the lettering on the box.

Lenore: Damn you!

Bruce: And don't forget to do the bottom this time.

Actually, it took four coats of white paint to cover all the lettering completely. As she would sit, waiting for coats of white to dry, I suggested that she think of ways to symbolize nothing. I forgot all about calling for the attendant to come and pick her up. So did she.

Second Session

Lenore: I don't want to be here.

Bruce: No one does. A psychiatric hospital is not a fun place to go for a vacation.

Lenore: You're a smartass.

Bruce: I'm not kidding, Lenore. I know that you don't want to be here. The problem is, I think, you don't really want to be anywhere.

Lenore: So what do I do today, paint more white? I handed her the box.

Bruce: No, just tell me what you think of when you look at this box.
Lenore: I'm pissed off! (I handed her an old copy of *National Geographic.*)
Bruce: So look in this magazine and find a picture about being pissed off.

The photograph she chose was of a wrecking ball smashing into a ruined building.

Bruce: Is that something you feel or is it a hobby?
Lenore: I feel it, of course!
Bruce: Good. Glue it into the inside of the box.
Lenore: Anywhere?
Bruce: Anywhere you think it fits. Now look at the box. What does it feel like now?
Lenore: Sad.
Bruce: What color is sad?
Lenore: Dark blue.
Bruce: Decide where the sadness should go in the box and I'll show you how to mix dark blue. I want you to paint the sad place dark blue.

Over the next few weeks, for an hour a day, the box continued to be filled and covered as Lenore and I conversed and free-associated on her "nothingness/lostness." Images of pain and anguish gave way to nostalgia. Themes of love emerged as she attempted to symbolize her two sons. As their representations were affixed to the box, thoughts of Little League football games, sewing and teaching and myriad other interests resurfaced. Lenore did a small piece of stitchery which she fastened to one side of the exterior of the box. This rekindled an old desire to design her own quilt. On an off-grounds trip to the library, she checked out a book of Amish quilt patterns. The last time I heard from her she was well into the work on the "quilt of her life." She has gone back to her home, back to being the mother of two sons and I believe she has rediscovered her own identity. She is no longer lost, for through her art she took the time to look for and find herself.

SOMEWHERE, SOMEBODY KNOWS THE ANSWER

In his existential novel *The Castle,*[7] Franz Kafka paints an eerie portrait of a man known only as K. It is K's strongest desire to enter and be welcomed as a member of the castle. This is not an easy task. K cannot find the gate, and the directions he is given by the authorities are vague and ambiguous. K is convinced that somewhere, somebody knows the answers. Surely there must be someone who could give him clear instructions for his quest. His frustrations and anguish over his repeated failures to gain access are excruciating. The reader is engulfed in a world of shadows and haunting echoes of one's own life in a world where nothing is absolutely certain.

At this point I could offer any number of illustrative vignettes of adult patients I have encountered in these past fifteen years. Many patients have come to me, as K does to the authorities, firmly believing that I know the answers and that I can tell them what to do. But I would rather tell you a part of my own journey.

My father died on January 1, 1953. I was eighteen months old, he was 41. He died of a heart attack. He had been wounded in World War II, and my mother says he was never quite the same after the war. When he died on New Year's Day, he left behind my three older sisters, my mom and me. I have no memory of him that I can claim as my own. I have family stories, that's all. Consequently, I have spent much of my life looking for fathers to adopt. I've looked to relatives, teachers, coaches and even religion. The question I framed unconsciously and asked indirectly of these father figures was, "Will you tell me what to do, so I can do it and assure my own acceptability?"

In 1973, as I began my internship in Art Therapy, I was sure that I had at last found my perfect father in the person of Don Jones, my supervisor. To me, this marvelous man was part magician, part guru, part living legend. I felt secure that here, finally, was someone who would tell me what to do. (This was essentially an unconscious process. It is only through years of struggle, supervision and therapy that I am willing or able to say these things openly.)

Midway through the yearlong internship I began to paint again at Don's insistence. For reasons I do not understand, I had done very little work artistically for one or two years before entering the program. The painting that grew over a few weeks plagued me (Fig. 1). One day I would look upon it with pride, the next day I found it repulsive. When the piece was nearly finished, I shared my ambivalence about it with Don. He suggested that I bring the painting to the student process group when I finished it. Not surprisingly, I both looked forward to and wished to avoid sharing the piece with my peers.

The painting is a montage of images centered around a large vertical eye. Many of the details I found personally interesting. One exception,

Figure 1. "One day I would look upon it with pride, the next day I found it repulsive."

however, was the section that was a reworking of a still life theme that I had painted dozens of times before.

When the student group gathered to work with my painting, I gave a brief overview of what I thought were the significant components. Describing the still life section, I said, "And this is just something I used to paint a lot. It really doesn't mean anything." I was irritated that when I had completed my synopsis, Don suggested we begin by focusing our attention on the still life. The images, as you can see in Figure 1 are a bowl of fruit, a wine bottle and a grimy American flag nailed to the wall. Don began by having me free associate on these images. I told him and the group that I thought this section related to my having been an objector to the Viet Nam War. I then suggested that we move on to more intriguing segments of the painting.

Patiently, Don returned to the still life images. He asked me to give the American flag a voice and to speak from its perspective. Talking for the flag, I began to sweat. Don asked, "Flag, how do you feel about having been nailed to this dirty wall?" The flag burst with anger toward the sonofabitch who had so defiled it. The more I spoke, the angrier I became. Finally I began to shake and couldn't speak at all.

In a gentle voice Don asked, "Bruce, have you ever seen that flag before?" I was stunned. I had indeed seen it before, not only in many of my paintings, but lying neatly folded in my mother's cedar chest. It was the flag that had covered my father's casket. I wept. Twenty-four years of loss, disappointment and anger came bubbling to the surface. Suddenly all the protest songs I had sung, the marches I had joined and the slogans I had shouted had little or nothing to do with conscious moral indignation over the Viet Nam War, and very much to do with feelings I had kept hidden away about growing up without a father.

My life has been forever altered by that painting. I no longer look to fantasy fathers for answers or validation of my worth. I have begun to work on fathering, myself. The addition of a son to my life, named Jesse after my dad, has helped. I am experiencing a genuine father-son relationship for the first time.

When I asked Jesse what he thought about doing art, he said, "It's good, and it's fun, dad." I agree that doing art is good, but it is not always fun. There is still no one who can tell me the answers.

Chapter IV

STRUCTURING CHAOS

Issues of structure, intentionality, spontaneity and freedom seem to emerge in a cyclic fashion in my work with students in the Clinical Internship in Art Therapy at Harding Hospital. Our students often come to us soon after having completed bachelor's or master's degrees in fine arts or arts education.

A common value for them is their investment in creative freedom. At times the structures and programs of the hospital environment appear oppressively restrictive and dogmatic. The interns bring their own set of developmental issues to the clinical program, but their struggle to understand the rules and expectations of the hospital is a vital one. This is the essential dilemma that all artists have as they prepare to work on a new piece. For that matter, it is the condition all face who approach the task of creating. To bring order to the chaos of material, to give form to the multitude of potentialities is the core of creative action.

Several years ago I went on a whitewater rafting adventure on the New River in West Virginia. The first rapids section on the trip is named *Surprise*. The river bends sharply, and suddenly there is a drop of ten feet or so. Then all is chaos for the next thirty seconds.

For about five minutes before we actually hit the rapids, we could hear the increasing roar. Then the bend, the drop, the chaos. It truly was a surprise. For a few moments I wondered if we would survive this "pleasure trip." On the second rapid I was thrown out of the raft. Although my life preserver did exactly as I'd been told it would and I made it through the rapid without so much as a scratch, I was shaking internally.

The whitewater is so overpowering that there is no way for a swimmer to have any control at all. All you can do is go with the flow. When the head guide ordered the company of eight rafts to pull over to the bank and prepare for lunch, I was still quivering inside.

It has been so long ago now that I have forgotten the guide's name, but at the time he seemed to me to be a cross between Tarzan and Superman. He climbed up on a large boulder to give instructions, "If you need to go to the bathroom, men upstream, ladies downstream. Now, we're going to have peanut butter and jelly sandwiches for lunch. . . . " He went on to tell us in some detail just how to create a PBJ. As silly as this sounds, the effect was marvelous. Here was someone in absolute control.

He was not wet, he was not frightened. I don't think he was even sweating. It was most reassuring to be told how to make sandwiches and where to go to urinate. He gave order to the swirling chaos of that morning on the river. Entering into therapy is not a placid experience for most people. The process of psychotherapy is painful and difficult, whether in its traditional verbal form or art psychotherapy, logotherapy or any of the other forms and techniques. Generally, people do not go out of their way to search for pain in their lives. The seeking out of therapy is an indicator of the level of turmoil the individual is experiencing. It is an acknowledgment that the struggle and discomfort of the therapeutic journey is perceived as necessary. In some ways the patient who initiates this journey is not so different from me as I floundered through the whitewater. The patients I treat often have felt themselves to be overwhelmed by the chaos of their emotional rapids.

It would have been no comfort at all if the guide had simply given us adventurers a pretrip lecture and then turned us loose on the river. It was essential that he go with us through that treacherous gorge. Still, he could do only his part of the work. Each of us had to do our share of paddling in order to navigate the New River. Our guide made no attempt to do it for us.

I believe it is the same with the patient who seeks the art psycho- therapy journey. If all I do is tell them the way or give them *my* truth and stand back and watch, it is doubtful that the necessary work would be done to ease their suffering. No journey would begin. Rather, I must make myself available to go along, to be with and be attentive to the patients as they explore the images that emerge from their depths. I do not fear this journey, nor do I fear their feelings, for they are only variations on the same themes I carry within myself.

To begin a work of art is to take a look in the mirror. Whether I do this literally or not, it is always the same. The canvas becomes a mirror that reflects who I am on the inside. David Ohm, when he was an art therapy intern at Harding Hospital, said, "The paper is always true. I look at it and see myself. It is so draining and nourishing."

To begin is always hard. There are so many possibilities. One always wonders what facet of self will be exposed this time. At a superficial level, this grappling with possibility is echoed in the decisions about gathering materials.

> What shape will the canvas be?
> What size?
> Gesso or rabbit skin glue?
> Oils? Acrylics? Water color?
> Monochromatic or polychromatic?
> Theme?
> Where to start—sketch or background?
> What techniques to use?
> etc., etc., etc.

The possibilities lend themselves to chaos, but at the same time the deeper issues of content are also forming. Each decision that the artist makes before starting to draw begins the process of structuring. As soon as the painter has decided the size and shape of a canvas, he has closed the door on myriad other choices. When he selects acrylics, other options dissolve. It is through the multiplicity of decisions, subtle and overt, that the artist begins to give form to the chaos of endless possibilities.

The same narrowing of attention, focusing, occurs in relation to subject matter as well as with raw materials and media. Envision a pyramid. At its base are the billions of visual, imaginal possibilities. These may be conscious or preconscious for the artist. As the time prior to the initiation of the task passes, the thematic selection process rises from the base to the tip of the pyramid and the painting is begun. The selecting and filtering process is energized by the psyche of the artist, powered by inner conflict, anxiety or other emotions. In most instances the thematic material that emerges is both deeply significant to the artist and safe enough to be expressed.

Exactly how this selecting/filtering happens is a mystery. I can most clearly conceptualize it in the image of boiling a pot of seawater. As the water boils and turns to steam, it eventually leaves a residue of salt. The salt was always there, but it took the boiling, churning and evaporating to make it visible. I believe that the same thing happens within the soul of the artist. Feelings, images, themes, conflicts and powerful forces simmer, and eventually the artist's "salt" is revealed as the artwork is completed.

The "salt" of a given art piece may never be verbalized by the artist. This often gives my colleagues who do not consider themselves to be artists a feeling of dis-ease. They want to force the essence of an art object into some verbal frame. Begrudgingly they accept the notion that art is nonverbal expression. This description is not satisfactory to me, since it defines the expressive quality of art in a negative way.

When I make this point, they will go slightly further and suggest the denotation of pre-verbal. Again, I protest! This suggests that the art process is in some manner a servant to words, as if the doing of art prepares one for speaking. This does violence to the art process. Those who force visual symbols into verbal constructs may be guilty of *imagicide*, i.e., the murderous destruction of an image.

If we must talk of art as somehow in relation to verbal communication, I suggest that artistic expression is meta-verbal. At this, my wordy friends turn their heads slightly and I see a look of tolerant compassion come over their faces. I interpret the look to mean, *Poor Bruce, he has climbed too far out on the limb.*

Even *meta-verbal,* suggesting a parallel process of equal or greater value than verbal, is a definition flattering to words, since it defines art images in terms of verbalizing. I propose that the essence of artistic expression cannot be described verbally, because the two modes of expression are inherently different. Words have to do with logical, rational connections. Art images have to do with psychic-salt which is often neither logical nor rational. They are simply different.

This is not to say that one or the other is of more value. On the contrary, I believe them to be of equal value. The doing of art by the artist, whether professional, amateur or patient, is a structuring of chaos at several levels. There is a parallel process at work as the artist focuses attention on the spectrum of decisions about material, media and size. Simultaneously, the psyche is filtering—boiling—selecting the theme that is most ready, most in need of emergence.

Chapter V

EXISTENTIAL EMPTINESS AND ART

The art psychotherapy journey is a difficult and treacherous one. It is often painful and frightening and almost always uncomfortable and anxiety-producing. The specific events and situations that lead, push or pull an individual to seek this journey are as varied as the individuals themselves. One common theme revealed time and again is existential emptiness.

Existential emptiness is a pervasive phenomenon in the twentieth century. Many factors have contributed to its development. The increased mobility of our society has had dramatic impact on the extended family. Few children today grow up in the hometown of their parents, much less their grandparents. Divorce has become commonplace and the one-parent family is no longer atypical. In the past thirty years there have been significant shifts in the practice of religions. All over the world there have been major challenges to governmental authority and a pervasive sense of skepticism about the motives of even the most virtuous nations on the globe.

Men and women have experienced the loss of their groundedness. Foundations and traditions have lost meaning, even to the extent of a sense of ahistoricity. There is no longer a familial tradition to tell one what to do or to invest certain acts with significance, or to model meaningful engagement in life. The result is a hedonistic, self-centered and shallow view of life and the world. This is reflected in the titles of popular magazines of the past few decades. They have shifted from *LIFE* to *People* to *US* to *Self.* One can envision future periodicals titled *Id* or *Impulse.* The Beatles commented on this trend in one of their last collaborations, the chorus of which is "I, me, me, mine."[8]

Existential emptiness often manifests itself in a vague sense of boredom. In the past ten years my clinical work has focused intensely on the treatment of adolescents. Boredom is the complaint heard most often. Adolescents whose behavior is disturbed and disturbing enough to bring them to the hospital carry with them a host of psychiatric labels. The jargon of these clinical descriptions, such as *borderline personality, severe adjustment reaction, conduct disorder,* are helpful in aiding the staff in understanding what has been happening in the lives of their patients prior to their seeking treatment. They do little, however, to address the internal sense of abandonment and loss, or absence, of meaning that the patient experiences.

The term "couch potato" describes the sort of depression that overtakes those who live their lives devoid of meaning beyond school or job. Denoting one who takes root on the couch and watches the routines of television throughout the evening and weekend hours, "couch potato" is a sadly humorous expression of emptiness. Perhaps television has replaced religion as "the opiate of the masses" as described by Karl Marx. Existential emptiness may also be understood as the underlying phenomenon that leads to drug and alcohol abuse, juvenile delinquency, mid-life crisis and the frequent rapid deterioration of those who retire from their life's work.

If we understand existential emptiness to be at the core of many of the dysfunctions our patients bring to us, we are left with the dilemma of what to do as therapists to help the patient. In a lecture at the Ursuline College in Cleveland, Ohio, Shawn McNiff emphasized that the root of the word *therapy* is "to be attentive to." For an existential art therapist the question is how to be attentive to the emptiness of the patient. Obviously, no therapist can give meaning to the life of the patient. The meaning of life is not consistent from person to person and, in fact, changes within the same individual over time. What is important is engaging not in intellectual discussion of universals but the here-and-now meaning of one unique individual's life at the present time.

To ask about the meaning of life in a general manner is somewhat like a question I posed to Don Jones many years ago. At the time I was an apprentice of sorts to Don, who was then the president of the American Art Therapy Association. As we sat in his office late one afternoon, I asked, "What is the most significant painting you've done?" He thought for a moment and then replied, "The next one." His answer to my earnest question irritated me, since I was so clear in my own mind which of my paintings was the most significant. Alas, it escapes me now just which painting that might have been. The simple truth is that there is no such thing as the most significant painting by a given artist. The importance of any work is always relative to the time and situation from which it emerged. The same can be said about human life. We each have our own unique purpose or mission. It is through this that we are known and because of this that we are irreplaceable in the world.

At every twist and turn of our lives we are challenged to solve problems and thus discover the meaning of our lives. Doctor Viktor Frankl suggests that it is a fallacy for any man to ask, *What is the meaning of my life?* Rather, he asserts, "Each man is questioned by life; to life he can only respond by being responsible."[9]

It is the essence of the existential art psychotherapy pilgrimage to be attentive to the patient/pilgrim who journeys inward toward discovery of his or her own responsibleness. The great struggle in this for both the therapist and the patient is that the patient is left alone to make the decisions about to whom or to what to be responsible. I have often been tempted to impose my own values or perspective, and yes, own meanings. My resistance to this temptation is at times a source of judgments on the patient. To do so would rob the patient of the discovery and to discredit my conflict between me and the patients. They seem so interested in my values, my judgments, that my efforts not to contaminate their journey are sometimes interpreted as withholding. I can counteract this perception by continually valuing their quest, in spite of their anger toward me.

Existential art psychotherapy is not a disguised cognitive teaching or re-teaching device. It does not make the mistake of the aforementioned airplane pilot attempting to instruct the ignorant. Its essence is in the visual image, which is often well removed from logical reasoning. It does not attempt to preach any moral code. It encourages creation of a personal system of ethical decision making. The photographer gives a portrait of the world from one perspective; the artist/therapist, in concert with the patient, offers multiple visions of the world as experienced by the patient. There is no need for imposition of my values or judgments, for if I genuinely engage the patients in the journey, their lives' images will offer their own truth.

In asserting that people are responsible and that if they are to have any sense of peace they must struggle to fulfill the meaning of their lives, it must be emphasized that I do not see this as a purely inner phenomenon. Meaning or fulfillment cannot be discovered in the isolation of the individual psyche any more than expressions of love can be found in masturbation. Meaning is located in the context of relationship to others. The "I, me, me, mine" approach to life will always leave the individual empty in the end.

To this point I have addressed the transitory nature of meaning. It changes from person to person and from day to day within any one person. Still, I insist it must always be present. As an existential art psychotherapist I believe that we can be genuinely attentive (therapeutic) to the patients in their journey by (1) doing with them, (2) being open to them, and (3) honoring their pain. These three tenets form the basis of my encounters with patients.

DOING WITH THEM

My clinical work in the inpatient setting might well be divided into two basic categories. One is the formal process of art psychotherapy, whether in a one-to-one primary therapy relationship or in a group. The other is more akin to a fine arts quest. It is this second category, *questing*, that I will discuss in relation to the "Doing with Them" tenet of existential art psychotherapy.

It begins as a patient is escorted through the door of the Creative Arts building. They frequently are frightened and uneasy. They often have only recently been admitted to the hospital. Many of their freedoms have been taken away. Their world has been chaotic and painful to such an extreme degree that hospitalization has become the best course of action. In the admissions process they have felt truly out of control, or at least out of options. They bring this burden with them as they enter the studio. It is a heavy burden, laden with anger, embarrassment and vulnerability.

The first few sessions are spent in relatively routine tasks that "everyone does when they're new." The specifics are less important than is my own engagement in whatever art task I am beginning of our work together. By my authentic and evident focus on my own currently caught up in. This is the work I begin to engage the patient in the metaphor of journey. It is important in these early encounters that I allow my frustration with a piece, the struggle with composition or dissatisfaction with some technical element to be seen. My struggle charts the course for the work we will do together on the journey. The doing of art is my ritual, a reenactment of my personal journey. My willingness and enthusiasm for the ritual is contagious and it both afflicts and affirms, challenges and assures the patient that the journey is worthwhile.

Sara

When Sara came into the hospital, her parents described her problems with drinking and substance abuse. She had been unruly and unmanageable at home and she had made two superficial attempts to kill herself. Sara's description of her difficulties was that no one was able to understand her and that she was "sad over the pointlessness of everything." Until fairly recently she had done quite well in school and for most of her seventeen years she had been an active and social girl. Her mother thought that Sara's current problems started when her parents divorced. The marriage had not been a happy one, but there was not a great deal of turmoil or ill will, according to Sara's mother. The divorce had been a friendly one, she said, that did nothing more than make public the distance between the couple. Two years later, she remarried. The new husband said that he and Sara had just never gotten along.

Sara was passive and bored for the first few weeks in the hospital. Her first projects in the creative arts studio were mediocre at best. At the time, I was working on a painting of a field in the middle of which a crumbling brick wall is connected to a door frame with a wooden door standing ajar. My first encounter of consequence with Sara came when she looked up from her table, where she'd been dozing, and asked, "Where does the door lead?" (Fig. 2).

I paused, stepped back from the canvas and replied, "I'm not sure . . . it's sort of scary, though."

She asked, "Then why did you paint it?"

"Because I had to." Sara wanted to know what that meant.

"I had to," I said. "This image just kept coming to mind. It wouldn't go away. I finally decided the only way to get it out of my mind was to paint it."

Sara said, "But it still bugs you."

"Yes," I responded, "it bugs me."

The next day Sara began the session by announcing that she was tired of all this dumb crap that she'd been doing. "I want to paint." I told her I'd be glad to help her any way I could, on one condition. She had to agree to stick with the task of painting for at least two months, no quitting. Sara agreed and we began by stretching her first canvas. As we worked, I said, "Another thing you'll have to do, Sara, is trust me as we go along these next couple of months."

Sara recoiled, "I don't trust anyone, and certainly not someone on the staff."

Figure 2. "Where does the door lead?"

I replied, "Well, you're going to have to try. It's hard to learn to paint. If you don't trust your teacher, it's almost impossible."

"Well," she said, "I'm not going to trust you and I'm not going to kiss your ass and tell you that I do."

Calmly, I told her, "You've got to get that left side tighter. Pull harder. By the way, that's a good sign, not lying to me. Relationships are built on honesty and trust. We've begun."

Sara grimaced and her knuckles whitened as she tightened the canvas and I stapled it secure. "I don't want any relationships and I don't trust you! What am I going to paint?"

"Well, right now you're going to gesso the canvas and then let it dry. We'll start painting tomorrow."

"But I want to start today," she whined.

At this, I quoted The Rolling Stones, "Well you can't always get what you want."[10]

Sara walked in the next day and waved a rough sketch in front of my face. "This is what I'm going to paint. It's so deep."

"No," I said, "I've thought about it and I want you to start by painting a still life. In fact, I want you to paint this vase." I held up an ugly, squat-looking, grey-blue ceramic vase that had been sitting around the studio for as long as I could remember.

"Oh, god, that's atrocious," she moaned.

"Perhaps, but it is the subject of your first painting."

After several minutes of protest, Sara grumbled, "Where do I start?"

"What color is the background?" I asked.

"Pure black," she snarled.

"Then begin by painting the entire canvas black."

"That's stupid."

"Trust me," I said.

Over the next three weeks Sara worked, painted over and re-worked the painting of the ugly vase, all the while stockpiling techniques such as overlay, wash, dry brush; learning the tricks of highlighting and shadow casting. Several times she threw down her brush and stomped off, but after a time she always returned. On one occasion, she announced that she was finished. Without commenting, I suggested she put a bit more emphasis on her highlight and darken the shadow on the opposite side. When she completed those alterations she decided she wanted a horizon line so the vase could appear anchored in space rather than floating in blackness.

The overall effect of her painting was crude, yet subtly haunting. In relation to content, I believe that what needs to be expressed will be, regardless of the subject. Other than focusing attention on the vase itself, I gave no limitation or instruction to Sara. What she created was a painting in black, white and mottled grey-blues of an empty vase sitting on an empty plane before a blank grey-black wall. The emotional import of this piece is isolation, dullness and boredom. It is both simple and poignant, an eloquent statement of how Sara felt about herself and her life at the time. Most important, she had experienced, at a meta-verbal level, her own ability to struggle—with the act of painting, with herself and with me.

During the following six months of intensive inpatient treatment, Sara completed approximately twenty-five paintings. In the same period I finished five or six of my own works. We argued now and then over technical details and at times engaged in heated conflicts when she would accuse me of being too demanding. I would respond by wondering out loud what she was avoiding. Through the months we developed a genuine relationship that tolerated the full range of feelings.

In her last session before discharge, while Sara was putting the finishing touches on a painting she titled *Saying Goodbye,* I asked her what she thought she'd learned while in therapy. Without missing a beat, she said, "I learned to struggle."

I chuckled and said, "Really?"

Sara replied, "Trust me."

BEING OPEN

A recurring, disturbing question all therapists must wrestle with is our level of transparency with our patients. What to share, when to share, boundaries, professional identity and personal integrity swirl together and gradually come to focus on openness between therapist and patient. There are several schools of thought surrounding therapeutic transparency.

I have changed my position more than once over the past decade and a half. In the early days of my career I was very interested in the philosophical writings of Carlos Castenada. Under that influence I kept my personal history to myself. This promoted a mystery of sorts onto which patients projected freely. This stance, however interesting to me, went against my basic nature and need for relationship and connection. It was gradually discarded as I became more comfortable with my role as therapist.

I have known therapists who had few or no professional boundaries. In contrast, I have also known colleagues for whom even the smallest of interactions with patients and professional peers was given intense scrutiny under the boundary spotlight. One such colleague used to irritate me, for he would not speak if we happened to pass each other on the hospital grounds. His view of our relationship was that it existed within the bounds of designated meeting times and places. While I did not like this treatment, I did learn to respect it because I was sure that he had his own set of well-thought-out reasons for maintaining his borders so rigidly.

Another colleague is less encumbered by such issues. This person has taken patients and ex-patients to dinner and similar social occasions. Clearly the latter is different from the former, but both have had good outcomes in treatment.

These extremes represent the opposing poles on a continuum of possible interactive styles between therapist and patient. In a deeper sense, this is true of all relationships, whether personal or professional. If we regard birth as our first encounter with distance and separation, then being placed on mother's belly is the first encounter with reconnection. This is one of the dominant metaphoric themes of our lives. From birth we constantly negotiate our distance and closeness, our individual integrity and our interdependence.

I believe that people discover meaning in their lives by being open to another. Meaning is not an exclusive process. Viktor Frankl points out time and again that meaning is found in self-transcendence, not self-actualization. He goes so far as to assert that "self-actualization cannot be attained if it is made an end in itself, but only as a side effect of self-transcendence."[9] All therapists, regardless of school or discipline, want their relationships with their patients to be meaningful. Clearly if the patient fails to invest the relationship with value and importance, there is no hope for growth or change in the patient as a result of the relationship. And so we return to the question of transparency.

The tools of my trade are metaphor, the artistic task and my willingness to be with the patient on the journey. The patient's task is to share his or her own story with me through art. Our identities are a compilation of personal history and the norms, myths and cultural meanings of the time in which we live. The art psychotherapy journey is a joint venture in sharing our tales through art.

Doctor Sheldon Kopp offers this view of the therapy process. "The contemporary pilgrim is a person separated from the life-infusing myths that supported tribal man. He is a secular isolate celebrating the wake of a dead God. . . . Today each man must work at telling his own story if he is to be able to reclaim his personal identity."[4]

When the patient starts his art psychotherapy journey, he embarks on an excursion into painful artistic expression that depends on his willingness to share the sights. The more the story is told, whether through drawing, painting, poetry or song, the more it is owned and understood. The painting of one's own life establishes the artist/patient as the creator of the story. It puts the patient in a position of power—power to accept, to internalize or externalize, to alter or even paint over the story. The deepest aim of arting out the story is to empower the artist/patient to grasp fully the meaning of his story. Viktor Frankl quotes Jean-Paul

Sartre: "Man invents himself. He designs his own essence . . . including what he should be or ought to become."[9]

The artistic process affords the patient an opportunity to create the meaning of life. The poignancy of this is heightened by the transitory nature of creating. Lack of permanence is reflective of the temporal quality of an individual's life meaning. When I look back on a painting I completed seven or eight years ago, I can still find great worth in it for what it means to me now, but I am most aware that it does not mean now what it did in years past.

The creative act is not an end in itself. It is not enough simply to paint or dance or sing in solitude. There has to be someone who can see the drawing, watch the dance or listen to the song. The other need not always understand, but must understand and I believe they must care.

As an art therapist in an inpatient setting I generally do not have the luxury of selecting my patients. Even given that opportunity I would be reluctant to turn down a request to treat a patient, regardless of my initial impression of how it might go. There have been many times that my first reactions to a patient have been negative, but, over the course of time in our shared journey, these same patients and I have developed significant relationships. I have learned not to be too cautious in approaching a new patient; that my reservations most often have to do with my fears about entering into a new relationship and very little to do with the patient's potential for growth. To work with patients to whom I am not initially drawn provides an opportunity for self-discipline, as well. It might be easier to work only with those patients to whom I took an immediate liking, but this would stultify my own struggle with life.

Each moment I spend with a patient, doing art and allowing relationship, is significant for me as well as the patient. I have chosen this as my life's work. Actuarily, I stand at the midpoint of my life. I am gradually becoming aware of the value of my time. I watch my children and mourn the passing of their infancy and preschool years. My time is moving very quickly. Within the past year my father-in-law died. It was not an easy death. He had suffered for several years from Alzheimer's disease and cancer. His death was a reminder of the ultimate aloneness of each human being. No one could go with him on his long journey. In spite of all the support and love of my wife's nine brothers and sisters, nothing could take away my mother-in-law's pain. She had to bear it alone. My own life has had its share of losses and scars, situations I neither wanted nor planned but was powerless to avoid. Granted, I have designed some of my misfortunes all by myself; but others have befallen me quite randomly. These experiences remind me ruthlessly of the transience of my life and how precious is my time.

As the art psychotherapy journey unfolds, it becomes apparent quickly to the patient and to me that if we are to get anywhere, we must both work. Not only must the patient draw out his story, but I must do the same. We need to know and trust each other. When I ask the patient to summon the courage to look in that emotional mirror, I must ask myself to do the same. I am constantly reminded to be honest. When I permit the patient to witness my struggle with the feelings aroused by my images, he is encouraged to openness and self-revelation.

My clinical interns ask how to know when and what to share. My most comfortable response is that they must experience the emptiness of missed opportunity when they withhold from a patient, and the pain of being abused by the patient who was not ready or worthy of the gift of their vulnerability. They must feel these emotions many times before they will gradually learn to listen to the internal cues that push them to reveal or warn them to retreat. It has been several years since I have contended with the personal pain of having revealed too much or too little. I have learned to accept my feelings, to share naturally without deliberate effort to anticipate or restrict the impact upon the patient. I believe that sharing is a good thing that begets good in others more times than not. Patients in the early resistance stages of therapy occasionally question my motives. Usually it is expressed, "You are only doing this because you are paid to do it." There is no way to debate this provocative, devaluing maneuver, rather like the question, "Have you stopped beating your wife yet?" The patient is dismayed as I chuckle at the challenge. There is no way to respond but to continue to be accessible and open to the patient.

In sharing our journey's images, the patient's story is the primary focus. I have not sought out the patient for my own purposes. It is the patient who comes seeking meaning. Whatever structure or exercise, media or event I may have in mind on a given day, it is the patient who guides the journey, with a multitude of possibilities through a sea of feelings. Because some of my patients are truly in chaos, I often set the parameter of the session by stating a theme. Still, when groups are running well, all I have to do is ask, "What do we need to draw?" When working with individuals I seldom initiate anything at all. It is, after all, their treatment, not mine. I use the principle *seldom initiate, always respond.* I trust that the patients will bring to the session all that they are and will take what they can from it.

During a painful and difficult period of my life I had a dream that has taught me a lot about trusting the process. I found myself standing in the middle of a rushing stream. My task was to alternately push with the stream or against it, in an attempt to alter the speed of the water. Soon after, I did a painting of the scene and took it to my therapist. We worked with the image. He asked whether my efforts, strenuous as they were, made any difference in the speed of the stream. Sadly, I replied, "No, no difference at all." He noted that in the painting there was a picnic blanket spread out on the bank beside the stream. He wondered how it might feel to lie on the blanket and watch the water rushing by. I responded that it would be so peaceful . . . a relief. He asked, "So why do you push so hard?"

The art psychotherapy journey begins when I meet the patient openly. The first steps are always the hardest, because I must be open to myself. I look in the creative mirror and give myself permission to see and to be seen. Sometimes the reflections are ugly, mean, malevolent. Sometimes I am awed by the courageous, loving things I see. I am part monster, part hero; part hater, part lover, and I allow myself to see them all. Through this artistic looking inward I have come to see myself as a prism, facet after facet, edge upon edge.

When I can be open to the prismatic reflections that emerge on paper, I am no longer at the mercy of those around me. I have nothing to fear from what they may see if I have already seen it myself. Doctor Henry Leuchter, a psychiatrist friend, has said, "Out of every ten people you meet, two will like you no matter what you do; two will hate you no matter what you do. The rest are up for grabs." This is the dilemma for the patient. If meaning in their lives must be found in the context of relationships, they (and I) must suffer the risk of being known.

As the images move from soul to canvas, they offer a new sense of possibility and responsibility. The artist who shapes and discovers the meanings of his life is empowered at the same time to change the picture if he chooses. Some works of art stand quite well on their own; others need to be reworked. Some cry out to be discarded; others demand exhibition. The creative act summons responsible ownership. I do not attack another's work as we journey together and I reserve the option to claim my privacy if need be. I do not expect to have to defend myself, nor would I use a battering ram on a patient's internal door.

These are the boundaries within which I create, discover and share meanings with my patients. Our journey leads us through a gallery whose walls are cluttered or graced with images of struggle.

A Story of Openness

Several years ago I began an expressive psychotherapy group as co-therapist with Doctor Carol Lebeiko, a child psychiatrist. The group consisted of six adolescent girls, each of whom had been diagnosed with adolescent borderline personality disorder. Although Doctor Lebeiko had no formal art or art therapy training, she had initiated the group because of her sensitivity to these patients and her frustration that other elements of the treatment program were not having the therapeutic impact she felt was necessary. Each girl brought her own painful, sometimes horrific history. Five of the six were from broken homes; four were adopted. They all had deep feelings of abandonment, inadequacy and rage.

I am cautiously skeptical about diagnostic labeling, but the description of borderline personality as a clustering of symptoms can be helpful. All six of our original group members were intense in their styles of relating. Their defensive use of splitting, projection, idealization and devaluing kept them well insulated from the interventions of the treatment team. In theory, the development of these defenses and the related feeling states of abandonment depression can be traced to early developmental stages, i.e., the initial separation/individuation phase. The progression from symbiosis with mother through the separation phase is determined in large part by the emotional climate between mother and child. It is not surprising that the six severely disturbed girls immediately focused intense feelings on Doctor Lebeiko. She became the here-and-now representative focus of years of hurt, disappointment, loss and anger. These are difficult enough to sort through in one-to-one therapy. In the group, the girls seemed to feed one another. The bile and venom would boil over, most often landing on Doctor Lebeiko.

Carol and I gave much time and attention, both before and after the group sessions, to strategizing how to move the girls past this fixated position. She often urged that we become more verbal and offer more interpretation of what we saw happen in the group. I agreed, although it is not my most comfortable way of working, and for a period of time we focused heavily on verbal interpretive interventions. It had no discernable effect on the caustic barbs the girls threw at her. Truly, if the patients could have spit acid, I believe they would.

This came to an abrupt halt, however, about six months into the life of the group. The drawing task of the day was to *symbolize an important day in your life.* Carol's drawing portrayed herself as a figure in white holding an infant. Several other figures were in attendance, looking at her. Telling the story of her drawing, she said it was the day her first child was born, a wonderfully happy occasion. As the group talked with her about the drawing, one girl asked why all the people in attendance were drawn in black. Doctor Lebeiko's face went white and she lost her breath, as if she had been hit in the belly. There was a long pause. I felt the group sense the poignancy of the silence. I had a fleeting image of buzzards circling a wounded animal. What followed is to this day one of the most remarkable moments I have ever experienced in a group.

Speaking quietly, Carol shared with the group that this was indeed a drawing about the birth of her first child, but not the wonderful occasion she had described at first. This was a drawing of the birth of a child who was born dead—her first child. Tears slid slowly down her cheeks. The girls were weeping silently, too, and so was I. One girl broke the silence by wondering out loud if her real mother ever cries for her. Another shared the anguish she felt as she said goodbye to her own baby when she gave it up for adoption.

No buzzards flew in for the kill. For a brief period of time these six angry, isolated bad girls experienced themselves as supportive, caring pilgrims. Doctor Lebeiko was no longer an ogre, a non-person. She became someone with whom they could cry...someone who would understand. The group was forever changed by Carol's transparency. I was, too.

HONORING PAIN

Not long ago I was preparing a presentation for a small private psychiatric hospital in upstate New York. Part of the paper dealt with cultural imagery. To open myself to the images around me, I listened to the radio, watched television and read newspapers and magazines with special care. These elements of our everyday existence are so common that it took some discipline to really look at, listen and digest the images presented. I tried to imagine myself seeing, hearing and experiencing each of these for the first time. It is impossible to divorce oneself totally from a lifetime of enculturation, but I did find myself being more attentive to the messages. This was discomforting.

As an art psychotherapist I believe that all things we create as individuals or as a society are partial self-portraits. During my period of hyperattention to public media I was particularly perturbed by what emerged as a corporate and individual view of pain and discomfort. A multitude of communications told me that pain was to be avoided at all cost. The messages came, sometimes subtle, sometimes blatant. Listen: there are hundreds of medications to relieve headaches, menstrual cramps, sore back and indigestion. Soap operas encourage relieving marital stress through extramarital affairs. A lawyer advertises easy divorce. Deodorant advertisements warn that no one should ever see you sweat, i.e., be uncomfortable. You can buy pills to make you sleep. You can buy pills to keep you awake. In some magazines you can send away for a spouse or lover, C.O.D., of course. On and on it goes. The deeply disturbing message underlying these, and many more, is that no one should have to endure discomfort or pain. No one should have to struggle. Life should be easy, and fun, and happy.

This view of life, this devaluation of pain is one of the major obstacles in our patients' search for meaning in their lives. One of the primary tasks of the existential art therapist, along with *doing with* and *being open,* is to bring a sense of *honor to the pain* of the patient. This is a difficult task, for it goes against our culture. To honor, to value the pain of another is, of course, to value one's own pain. This presumes that our ultimate concern is not self-gratification or hedonistic pleasure but to understand the depths of our own meaningful existence. I believe that this is why so many people in the helping professions view their mission as alleviating discomfort. It is a sublimated attempt to ease their own misery. I propose a different view. As an art therapist I do not try to make someone feel better; I do try to help them understand, to discover the deeper gift of their feeling bad. Often, this helps the patient feel more at ease, less anxious, less pained, but that is a pleasant side effect, the icing on the cake.

As existential art therapists we have a sacred task to enact with patient. Viktor Frankl and I agree with Nietzsche's assertion, "He who has a *why* to live for can bear almost any *how.*"[9] I claim this task is sacred, for *sacred* calls up ideas of spirit, holiness and devotion, in contrast to technical formulations, cognitive constructs and behavioral interventions so often written about in our time.

In *Man's Search for Meaning,* Doctor Frankl recalls that Jean Paul Sartre wrote that man invents himself, designs his own essence, chooses what he should be or ought to become.[9] Viktor Frankl subtly alters this by asserting that the meaning of our existence is not invented by ourselves; rather it is detected.[9] The art psychotherapy journey is an effort to detect or discover the meaning of life by exploring the soul of what we invent in our creative work.

Essential in the explorative creative process is the therapist's belief that pain is not a malady to be banished but a reality to be embraced. The capacity of the therapist to honor the pain of the patient hinges on the therapist's attitude toward his or her own suffering. The shaman gained authenticity by going on his own inner pilgrimage and surviving, giving the seeker confidence in the shaman. The therapist who would bring honor to the pain of another must first honor his own pain. In *Man's Search for Meaning,* Frankl states, "Whenever one is confronted with an inescapable, unavoidable situation, whenever one has to face a fate which cannot be changed . . . just then is one given a last chance to actualize the highest value, to fulfill the deepest meaning, the meaning of suffering. For what matters above all is the attitude we take toward suffering, the attitude in which we take our suffering upon ourselves."[9]

To bring honor to our pain or the pain of another is, in the most radical sense, to shift from the position of victim to the position of hero. This is an empowering process that embraces life as it is. While many art therapists portray their mission as having to do with resolving conflicts, brightening affects or altering negative behavior, the existential art therapist does not exclude these but goes beyond by accompanying the patient on a journey that restores dignity to pain.

Faces in the Trash:

Dee was suicidal when she was admitted to the hospital. Because of the severity of her acting-out and suicidal episodes, she was confined to the living unit for a long time and was often in special care and restraints. After several months she had stabilized enough that her treatment team wanted to begin to allow her some off-unit treatment experiences. While confined to the unit she had often drawn spontaneously. Her drawings were gruesome, horrific images which both intrigued the cottage staff and made them uneasy. She was referred to my adult expressive group. It is my custom to let the group know a new patient is coming, at least a session or two ahead of time. When I told the group that Dee had been referred, there was a flurry of protest. Her reputation for explosive unpredictability had been heard throughout the hospital. Everyone had heard stories of her violent outbursts. Dee was a boiling pot of rage and pain.

Very early in her journey with me, Dee defined, through her drawings, what would become the dominant recurring symbols of her quest for meaning. She drew the masks she wore: frightening, angry, charming and wounded. She drew images of people crumpled in the bottom of a trash can. She drew walls that protected and smothered her. And she portrayed an inner cavern where an infant cried for its mother.

These metaphors were drawn or painted over and over in more than a hundred pieces of art. My response was one of consistent, matter-of-fact acceptance, despite the anxiety she stirred in the group and in me. (I, too, had heard of Dee's reputation.) As our relationship grew I introduced a metaphor of my own: that people are like prisms with facet upon facet. I emphasized how important I thought it was to express all facets of ourselves—the beautiful and ugly, the warm and cold, the angry and afraid. All of these are valuable, essential pieces of self.

The source of Dee's suffering was her sense of abandonment in the world. She had been born to a mother who was unprepared to care for a child. Eventually, she was adopted by her grandmother, who took good care of Dee in a physical and material way, but was unable to give her the essential nurturance as she grew. In a deep sense, Dee was aware of her aloneness in the world and this fed her rage and self-loathing. Her rage intimidated others and solidified her isolation. So the painful cycle went.

A most difficult moment in the life of the group came on a day when Dee had received a letter from her mother. She entered the room oozing hostile energy. The drawing task of the day was focused on giving symbolic messages to others in the group. As I set the structure for the session, Dee relaxed a bit and seemed to cool. She calmly drew a burning lightning bolt, an ice cube, an empty glass and a blue baby's blanket. When all had finished drawing, I asked if there was any need to share our images with words to one another. Dee stood up and pointed at one of her peers, saying harshly, "You are an angry bitch." To another, "You are frigid," to another, "You have nothing to offer anyone," and to another, "You are a helpless child." She summarized, "All of you mean nothing to me. I am throwing you all away." With that she began tearing the group's drawings off the wall. The group was stunned and I was furious. As she tried to throw the crumpled and torn images into the waste can, I stood and blocked her path. After seven months of intensive work, I felt that she was literally throwing it all away. For the first time I raised my voice, "Dee, I am not disposable! You can't get rid of any of us that way. I am a part of our relationship and so is everybody else in this room!"

She looked at me, quivering and wide-eyed. Then for the first time since I had known her, she began to cry. She turned and ran from the room. The rest of that session was spent in the group's dealing with what had happened. They did this with compassion and fairly profound insight. One of her peers said, "I never saw Dee vulnerable before. I think all those things she drew were really about herself."

I began the next session by talking about the notion of cherishing as it is described in Robert Heinlein's book *A Stranger in a Strange Land.*[11] The crux of what I said was that too often we discard or discount people and things around us without really knowing them. Perhaps we should take time to cherish what surrounds us. I asked the group to draw images of what they cherished in one another. Dee was hesitant at first, but then she drew a fiery lightning bolt, an empty glass, an ice cube and a baby blanket. As she later spoke of her drawings, she was warm with her peers.

After everyone had finished I suggested that perhaps we cherish these things in others because they remind us so of parts of ourselves.

Dee responded, "Yes, that's right. I am so angry all the time and I am cold. I feel so empty, like a baby left in some dark cave somewhere."

The level of sharing that followed in the group was wonderful. No longer a collection of infuriated, isolated women, they had become a band of pilgrims struggling to understand their pilgrimage. Near the end of the session, a member of the group turned to Dee and asked, "How did you feel when Bruce yelled at you the other day?"

Dee thought for a moment. "I felt like I was finding something and losing something at the same time. It was confusing. I wanted somebody to hold me like I was a little girl."

In the months that followed we got to know Dee's infant intimately. This abandoned, hurt and frightened child led the way as Dee journeyed back into the land of the living, out of the cave of those who would be dead. The more Dee learned about herself, the more she understood about others. In one of her last drawings she found herself cradling an infant in her arms, deep in the cave. There was little need for putting the experience into words. Dee just let the warm tears flow.

The existential art psychotherapy journey provided Dee with a *place to do,* to creatively express herself with the actions of art in the early stages of her treatment. As things progressed, she continued the *doing,* coupled this with *being with* others in a shared, accepting transparency. In the later phase of her inpatient therapy, the images of the abandoned, hurt child-self and Dee's adult nurturing (mothering) self became the dominant symbols. Dee began to experience the power of her vulnerability and the strength of her nurturing ability. She came to regard both facets as valuable gifts from their life to her life.

At a monthly *Coffee House* on the eve of her discharge, Dee sang a song she had written. As she finished, there was an intense silence. All in the audience were moved by Dee's gift to them.

> *Being lost and being cold*
> *So out of touch, so in control*
> *So mean and nice, like fire and ice*
> *A shell without a soul*
> *And hurting far too badly*
> *For anyone to know*
> *But deep inside the child cries*
> *Mom says, so it goes*
>
> *The fires burn, the memories churn*
> *Of tears and all the laughter*
> *The gentle hands, the pounding ones*
> *And all the mornings after*
> *And needing far too deeply*
> *Never knowing why*
> *But deep within, again and again*
> *Mommy sighs, don't cry*
>
> *To come of age with all the rage*
> *A stranger in the mirror*
> *Build the walls as heroes fall*
> *Live on pain and fear*
> *And wanting far too clearly*
> *For anyone to share*
> *And hidden there, beneath the tear*
> *Mommy scolds, don't care*
>
> *Being here and being there*
> *From black and white to graying*
> *To fill the cup and drink it up*
> *Try again at playing*
> *And finding far too slowly*
> *The stranger there is me*
> *I turned the page on monstrous rage*
> *And mommy set me free*

Dee has gone on in her life to earn a degree in an allied health profession. I suspect that she is skillful and sensitive in her work. I am sure that she is able to understand the pain of her patient and, in her own way, lead the patient to a deeper and more meaningful existence.

Chapter VI

THE FRAME OF THE CANVAS MIRROR

All of the various schools of thought and methodologies of therapy have at their foundations a theory regarding their practice. Underlying is a vision of how the therapist may best be attentive to those in need. Juxtaposed with the more technical or cognitive strains of art psychotherapy, the existential approach that I embrace is built from the philosophy of life presented by *logotherapy*. It is based on three fundamental assumptions that form a chain of interconnected links:

1. Freedom of Will
2. Will to Meaning
3. Meaning of Life

Freedom of Will

In the studio I watched as Rob put the finishing touches on a painting of heavy chains and a huge key-lock, on a black background. Rob said, "That's the way it is. The older I get, the more chains are wrapped around me." Rob speaks for many of his fellow human beings as well as for himself at this period in human history. He sees no possibility that he is free to choose his path. He sees no possibility that he is responsible for his life. Needless to say, he is not free from the circumstances of his existence, either cultural, sociological or psychological. But Rob is, as are we all, free to choose his attitude toward his circumstances. He is free to be a prisoner in his relationships, or a liberator. Humans are able to react and respond not only to the world but to themselves as well. We can reflect on our lives. It is the special condition of humans to manifest both self-consciousness and conscience. We can detach from ourselves and transcend the self. That we can go beyond the realms of physical presence is what defines us as human, as it allows us to delay pleasure in service to another. Our ability to detach, to observe ourselves is the special capacity that allows freedom within our limits.

The artist enacts the paradox of freedom and limitation, beginning with the ultimate freedom: to create whatever he wants or to do nothing at all. This freedom is chaotic and often is the most difficult barrier to cross. It is the decisions that follow, the structuring and limiting of possibilities, that bring freedom of action on a particular artistic work. Every decision— medium, technique, theme—paradoxically binds and liberates.

Writers complain of "writer's block," that feeling of being stuck, unable to type the first word. Artists experience the frustration of wanting to paint but being at a loss as to what or how to paint. In either case, it is the inability to limit oneself that paralyzes the creative flow. Once the boundaries have been established the freedom has begun.

Like Rob, I have found that as I grow older, more chains are draped across my back. Unlike Rob, I do not experience this as imprisonment but rather as opportunity to more clearly define the meanings of my life, my relationships, my personal and professional obligations. Occasionally I examine an individual link and find it rusted, more burden than worth. I may choose to disentangle myself, or I may decide to carry the burden anyway. Regardless of *which* I choose, *I choose.* Our chains are our ties to the earth, our anchors to life. On the one hand they limit; on the other they free.

The therapeutic task with Rob is one of empowerment. As we journey together, I pay close attention to his self-destructive self-limiting. I celebrate those moments when he owns his choices. Watching him paint, being with him as he struggles with beginning, offers a marvelous opportunity to explore with him his attitude toward the limits of his life in metaphor.

Bruce: You choose black as your background.
Rob: Yes, it's rather dismal, isn't it?
Bruce: It looks dark and heavy.
Rob: I guess it has to be that way.
Bruce: But you could have painted it red or blue or yellow.
Rob: No, it had to be black.
Bruce: (pointing to the paint cabinet) I see a jar of pink, even.
Rob: What are you trying to say?
Bruce: Only that you choose black.
Rob: It has to be.
Bruce: No, we have other colors.
Rob: What's your point?
Bruce: That you choose.
Rob: All right, damn it. I choose.

By owning that choice, Rob allows the possibility of other choices which might be quite different. In our journey together, this sets the recurring theme: that Rob need not be the victim, that he is free to choose, he has the power to choose.

Will to Meaning

The quest for meaning is crucial in the life of our patient as it is in our own. Reductionists argue that life can be described as the interrelationship of biological urges. Others suggest that our lives are little more than the compilation, layer upon layer, of habitual behavior patterns. Therapists who treat from such a philosophical base speak of the search for meaning as defensive intellectualization, or rationalization of drives. As an existential art therapist I do not discount the contributions of drive theories or behavior theorists. I do submit that there is more to the human being than habit and *id*. Meaning in life is one's own. Only the individual can discover it and fulfill it. Frankl states, "Only then does it achieve a significance which will satisfy his own will to meaning."[9] We must be cautious, however, that while on the one hand we assert that only the individual himself can fulfill his meaning, we remain aware on the other hand that meaning cannot be found within the individual in isolation. It is always found in the complex interplay of the searcher and others.

The role of art in this is profound. If we keep the image of the canvas mirror in mind, we have the paradox clearly illustrated. The artist, as he creates, struggles with his own conscious and unconscious depths to free the image and give it life on the canvas. The beauty of the canvas mirror is that it reflects not only the apparent reality but that which is hidden, from the past, and that which is longed for or feared in the future. Once the creative activity is complete—the painting signed and framed—its life, its significance depends upon the beholding by others.

When the artist has looked deeply into the canvas mirror and allowed the flow of imagery from self to proceed, he has said in the most honest of means, "This is who I am. This is why I am." Were he to drape the finished piece in translucent cloth and hide it away in some dark closet, he would proclaim, "I am nothing. I am pointless." This seldom happens. Whether professional, amateur or patient, the artist has a deep urge to have the work seen and embraced by others. This is the clearest of examples that our will to meaning is a force both intrapersonal and interpersonal.

Chapter VII

AN ARTIST'S VIEW OF MEANING

The middle-aged woman pushed her chair away from the table in the studio. She had just finished the patina on a small piece of sculpture. It was in the form of an open shell, very rough and crusted on the outside but smooth and well organized inside. Resting gently in the center was a small sphere. In a purely representational way it called up images of oysters and pearls. At another level it evoked a feeling of protection and safety mixed with vulnerability.

I admired the form.

Bruce: This is very nicely done.

Gwen: Oh, I don't know.

Bruce: I mean it. It's a powerful work. It must mean a lot to you.

Gwen: No, it's nothing at all. The lady (another therapist) told me I had to do something, so I did.

Bruce: Reminds me of oysters.

Gwen: (laughing) What?

Bruce: Really. Have you heard the story about how pearls are made?

Gwen: No.

Bruce: Well, you see, oysters get a piece of sand caught in the soft inner tissue and it hurts them. To ease the irritation they cover the piece of sand with a creative juice that makes it easier to tolerate. But then that gets hard, too, and it hurts. So the oyster coats it again. This happens many times over until what is left is a pearl. The ugly hurtful piece of sand is transformed by the creative juice and made beautiful.

Gwen: Is that the truth?

Bruce: Well, it may be a little poetic, but I do think it is true about art.

Gwen: How?

Bruce: It is often the things that hurt or are uncomfortable that artists are motivated by. I know for myself that I don't paint when I'm feeling great.

52

Gwen: Why not?
Bruce: I'm too busy feeling good. There's no reason to paint.
Gwen: So you only paint when you feel bad?
Bruce: Something like that.
Gwen: Does it make you feel better?
Bruce: Sometimes, but sometimes it makes me feel worse.
Gwen: That's the way this thing is. (She gently touches the piece.)
Bruce: It makes you feel worse?
Gwen: Yes, it makes me think of when my kids were little.
Bruce: And you protected.
Gwen: Yes, protected and fed and cleaned and loved and ... (tears run).
Bruce: They're all grown up now?
Gwen: Yes, they're gone.
Bruce: It's a beautiful sculpture.
Gwen: Thank you.

Artists have always known that a major source of their creativity is their own inner emotional turmoil. A character in one of Stephen King's novels, *Misery,* puts it this way:

"... Because writers remember everything ... especially the hurts. Strip a writer to the buff, point to the scars and he'll tell you the story of each small one. From the big ones you get novels, not amnesia. A little talent is a nice thing to have if you want to be a writer, but the only real requirement is that ability to remember the story of every scar. ... Art consists of the persistence of memory."[12]

Perhaps the purpose of art at its deepest level is to transform the scars of life; to take the painful piece of sand and create a pearl. This transformation represents and makes sacred the polarities in our lives. It allows the artist to synchronize with the natural flow of life. Nietzsche describes healing as an acceptance of conflict and struggle. The creative act is the transforming agent of these powerful forces.

It was a pleasure to watch the sculptress, Gwen, in her encounter with the rough, square block of stone. She had come to the hospital following a serious suicide attempt. At first she chipped aimlessly. Then, as she began to allow the image to emerge from the stone, her movements became more intentional, more precise. What started as a vague meandering gradually became a clear encounter between herself and the hammer, chisel and stone.

The observable change in her intensity while working was reflective of the deeper internal process as well. In the beginning she was aimless, noncommittal and detached. The harder she worked, the more directed she became. The form of the oyster and pearl emerged, speaking eloquently of her sadness about her empty nest. Her sculpting is both an external and an internal phenomenon. As she gives form to the stone, she likewise begins to mold the emptiness within herself, to master it. The most profound artistic works can be born only of such inner pain and transformation experiences. Art brings meaning to life by utilizing conflict and honoring painful struggles. The existential art therapist understands the essential nature of struggle and tension; how the collision of forces brings about the creative actions of art. Our primary task is to engender in the patient that same attitude towards their discomfort. We must transform the patient's view of self from that of victim to that of hero.

Through the artistic transforming experience the sculptress began to be able to affirm her opposites, the parts of herself that felt so vulnerable, and the parts strong enough to protect. Her internal contradictions and conflicts began to make sense as they became the well from which she drew her creative inspiration.

As humans we are a mass of opposites, contradictions and inconsistencies. In the process of continual change, conflict is inevitable. Whether we are able to accept our own changing, conflictual self secures or threatens our mental health. There is a basic tension within the self that is the manifestation of our internal polarities. The individual's response to these forces range from numbness to anxiety to creative working-through. Art does not diminish but utilizes the tension in empowering actions. The artist discovers meaning in life as he molds and honors the painful disharmony of his self. Creation does not ease but rather ennobles the pain. It does not cure, it accepts. Through the creative actions of art, contradictions and conflicts are brought into sharp focus that makes *non-logical sense.* Art embraces our deepest fears, loneliness, pain and guilt. Looking into the canvas mirror, the artist collides with pieces of self that are often distasteful and sometimes disgusting. On occasion the discoveries are pleasant, even beautiful. More frequently the expressions of my patients are clumsy, terrifying and raw. At such times, my task as therapist is to welcome the painful expressions as a gift, thereby to provide an atmosphere of security and empathy that encourages the heroic effort it takes to look at one's ugliness.

Therapists' meaning

The primary thrust of my work is to journey with the patients as they explore and discover the meanings of their lives, reflected in their creative work. In training interns, I stress that we should not be seduced into becoming merely interpreters, assessors or diagnosticians. I am not interested in training therapists to make clever technical interventions. I believe that if the necessary work is done by the patient as we walk together, he or she will make all the interpretations, judgments and alterations that are important. The changes will be lasting, since they emerge from the self, as opposed to any that are imposed by outside structure.

Chapter VIII

LISTENING TO THE IMAGE

Several years ago I worked with a woman who was hysterically mute. For several months she worked only in black chalk, refusing any other color or medium. In my clinical notes I often referred to her depression and the sadness reflected in her graphics. Much later, after she had regained her ability to speak and had worked through with her psychiatrist much of the trauma that had led to her muteness, I remarked casually about her depressing black drawings. She laughed, "Black is my favorite color and I like you a lot, so I used my favorite. . . . "

That was one of my first lessons in what not to do as a therapist. I had so easily allowed my bias about her use of color affect what I thought she was expressing, I had completely missed her intent.

Since then I have worked at disciplining myself in the art of listening to the image. It protects me from doing violence to an artist's work. My friend Shawn McNiff says, "The abuse of images and art works has to do with the implied negativity of the interpreter and the inability to approach the art object for what it is."[2] As I look back I can see the abuses I committed under the guise of my own omniscient approach to patients' works. It is paradoxical that as I have grown in knowledge and experience, I am much less sure of the meanings of specific images. I have become very careful not to commit *imagicide.* I am quite skeptical of my, or anyone else's, objective interpretive skills.

Beyond skepticism, I am no longer sure that there is any point of such an attempt in relation to art. An illogical extreme of "objective interpretation" was illustrated many years ago at one of the early national conferences of the American Art Therapy Association. In a workshop, a colleague described a style of working. Essentially, the patients brought completed paintings to the therapist's office and dropped them off at the secretary's desk. My colleague would analyze the piece, write a summary and the patient would be notified as to when the painting and analysis could be picked up. No dialogue, no relationship, no intimacy between patient and therapist. Within the framework of my work, such a style of interpretive analysis is a meaningless waste of time. It is in fact harmful to both the artist and the image.

I am uneasy, also, with those who argue that no interpretation is of consequence. I have a friend who is a fine painter. He is sometimes offended by my profession. His position is that the artwork stands for itself, by itself. His radical view is that to attempt any dialogue about the content of a work is to belittle it and its creator. He is not far from the position of Georgia O'Keefe, who tired of questions about her symbols. Alas, this cuts off the essential opportunity for poignant dialogue between artist and audience. The doing of art, in whatever form, is a call for engagement between creator and witness. In the period of give and take between the two lies the pathway to the emergence of meanings for both.

The artist brings his projections to the moments of engagement with the audience. Likewise, the observer brings his projections. The possibility for discovery or creation of meaning lies in the joint process of sorting through the projections; discarding some, accepting others and in the process creating additional ones that call for further sorting, and so on and so on. If taken seriously, it is an overwhelming task to interpret the art of another, or for that matter, of your own.

In the introduction of this book, I said I would not offer technical suggestions. Still, all rules cry out to be broken and I shall break my own by offering the following description of disciplined listening to the image.

As we deal with others, we must accept the fact that all therapists are subjects in their own right and therefore prone to projections. Therefore, rather than thinking about what a patient's image may mean, I have taken the opposite course. As I look at the drawing or painting, I try to exhaust the possibilities of meanings. While recognizing that this is impossible for me to do, I make the effort, in a highly structured way. The steps in this procedure are:

    1. Seeing—to see what is there
    2. Exploring symbols   INTERNAL
    3. Acknowledging feelings

    4. Listening to the story
    5. Retelling the story   EXTERNAL

Seeing — To See What is There

In the years that I have been training students, both at the Columbus College of Art and Design and in the Clinical Internship in Art Therapy at Harding Hospital, one of the most difficult lessons to transmit has been to see what is there. By this I mean to approach an art piece first as a non-rational visual encounter. For example, consider the painting in Figure 3. The intern, when asked, "What do you see?" begins as follows:

"I see a window and an apple and keys. . . . "

Figure 3. "It is all too easy for the interpreter to see the red shape on the right, label it Apple.."

But if we back up and really look at what is there, without regard for what it may represent in objective form, we begin to *see* the painting, rather than catalogue and label it. Such a seeing description of this piece might be:

"I see a large light blue field of color. It is broken by a greyish-brown

L-shape. I see several colors of blue and blue-grey. There is a section of very warm color—reds and oranges—on the right. These warm colors are echoed in smaller form on the far left and they are blended with a burnt umber shape. . . . "

With no mention of objects at all we have begun, just by listing the colors and shapes of things, to get a sense of what may be important later on in the process: the contrasting feel of the predominant blue-grey tones with the warmth of the oranges and reds. The purpose of this step is to gain a sense of what is literally there to be seen, without biasing notions of what objects may be represented.

Exploring the Symbols

If I have erred over the years in treating patients (and I am sure I have), the most common error would be to have succumbed too easily to my prejudice about a symbol. To minimize this likelihood, I discipline myself to explore as many of the possible meanings of a given symbol as I can.

Returning to the painting, it is all too easy for the interpreter to see the red shape on the right, label it "Apple," then leap to the symbol of the apple as a representation of the apple Eve gave Adam. I urge attempting to exhaust the possibilities:

Apple = Adam and Eve story
Apple = Knowledge
Apple = Isaac Newton and gravity
Apple = Taking one to teacher
Apple = The Beatles record label
Apple = Computers
Apple = Cider—fall—harvest
Apple = Core issues
Apple = Johnny Appleseed
Apple = Teacher's Pet
Apple = Sin
Apple = Sexuality
Apple = Nurturance
Apple = Pie and Motherhood
Apple = Tree, treehouse, childhood
Apple = Love, the apple of my eye

There are no doubt more symbolic meanings to apples. My point is that to do justice to the symbol of the apple the artist has painted, we must attempt to be as open to the multiplicity of meanings as we can. At the same time, we must allow the possibility that the apple is nothing more than an apple. This same openness must be applied to each of the objects portrayed in the painting. The window, the keys, the furniture spindle, the field, the ledge all hold the possibility of many different meanings that deserve unbiased attention.

Acknowledging the Feelings

As I sit in my office and look at this painting (Fig. 3), I am bombarded by the feelings it calls up in me. These change from time to time. One day I find myself staring through the window at a rather melancholy field that seems to go on for a long time. On a different day I am reminded of the warmth inside this room, in contrast to the cold outside. At other times I am fascinated by what those keys might open for me. There are moments when I can almost smell the apple pie baking in the unseen oven to the left of the window. Sometimes I wonder if I couldn't make a new story every time I look at this painting.

When I approach the work of my patient artist I try to open my emotional self to what he or she has created. I try to let myself feel the painting's emotions, whether explicit or subtly implied.

Seeing—to see what is there; exploring the symbols; acknowledging the feelings are internal processes. I try to do them before I utter the first word to the patient about the art. It is the first half of the interpretive experience. It is my half of the initial work. Its purpose is to provide me with a pathway into the life of the patient. Through the sorting and exploring of colors, lines, shapes, symbols and feelings, I move to engage the patient. Often the path is clear; at other times it leads me astray. In either case it is only a portion of the interpretive experience. The next two steps take place in the arena of dialogue with the patient. It may be verbal or active.

Listening to the Story

At this time in our history, we seem to have lost much of our appreciation for story telling and story listening. Perhaps the pace is too slow; we are so accustomed to the rapid flow of television. We get little practice in listening to an extended metaphor, a story. Some would do away with metaphor altogether, saying it only confuses the listener. Others see metaphor as decoration for speech, doing nothing to enhance the meaningful nature of our language. John Dominic Crossan, in his work, *In Parables,* asserts that participation metaphors are indispensable.[13]

" . . . metaphors can also articulate a referent so new or so alien to consciousness that this referent can only be grasped within the metaphor itself. . . . When a metaphor contains a radically new vision of the world it gives absolutely no information until after the hearer has entered into it and experienced it from inside itself."[14]

The existential art psychotherapy journey is much like story telling and story listening. Artworks are metaphors of participation, with the capacity to rearrange the view of the world, of self and others, for both artist and beholder. The sharing of their stories provides an opportunity for growth and change.

If the therapist has genuinely opened himself to the image of another, i.e., tried to see what is there, explored the potential symbolism and acknowledged the feelings the work evokes, he is ready to begin listening to the story as told by the artist. It is often helpful for the therapist to make an initial open-ended statement. Again in reference to Figure 3: "I find myself looking out the window wondering. . . ." This indicates interest in the scene, involvement in what is happening and interest in the plot. I avoid the who, what, when, why, how sort of questions, which quickly reduce the encounter to a reporter/interview experience, naturally calling up defensive responses rather than sharing depth experiences. The listening must be authentic, for nothing will shut down the exchange more quickly than the storyteller sensing disinterest on the part of the therapist listener.

The patient is often a person who has long been separated from the life-giving story-myths that offered support to earlier generations. Today it is difficult work to tell one's tale. Yet, it is in this sharing that the patient is able to rediscover his own identity, bring honor to his suffering and meaning to his life's journey. As the patient and I begin the artistic quest, we set upon an adventure in storytelling. The assumption is that the sharing of metaphors will lead to an understanding of self and others. This creative look at personal history can lead to transformation of the artist/patient from one who is imprisoned by the past to one who is enlightened by it.

The telling of the story, the creation of the art, is not, in itself, enough. The story must be heard, as the image must be seen by another. "But sometimes it is not enough for there simply to be another to listen. A man not only needs someone to hear his tale, but someone to care as well."[4] The ability to be open and secure enough to care is the special gift of the art therapist.

Retelling the story

In the foreword to his book, *Fundamentals of Art Therapy*, Doctor Shawn McNiff likens it to "a second poetic presentation. The first poetic experience is art therapy itself."[15] When I first read this, it crystallized for me what I have been doing with my patients for years, i.e., retelling their stories with stories of my own. As they paint, I paint. When they draw, I draw, and as they struggle to put into words the deeper meanings of their images, I share in the struggle. The journey becomes, in this sense, a mutual exchange of visual and verbal metaphors. Of course, the patient's story is always of most importance. They are after all the ones seeking and paying for my services. Still, I believe that the most validating experience I can offer my patients is to respond to their work with works of my own that resonate with and illuminate their struggle.

The Disciplined Listening

As an existential art psychotherapist it is always my deepest intent to help the patient in his or her process of self-discovery and fulfillment of meaning. Disciplined listening (seeing, exploring symbols, acknowledging feelings, listening to and retelling the story) protects me from doing violence to the images of my patients by interpreting their work in isolation. While I could certainly look at an object of art and hypothesize about the psychological content without knowing the artist at all, I refuse to do so. In my view, it would be a pointless intellectual exercise. Interpretation must always be an evolving, revealing dialogue between patient and therapist if it is to have genuine meaning and therapeutic value. To attempt to interpret an artist's work outside the context of relationship with the artist and without an empathic dialogue with and about the artwork, is to attempt to impose one's own meanings upon another. I can never accept this as valid or useful; rather, I propose we work strenuously at developing a disciplined approach to seeing and listening.

Chapter IX

DIMENSIONS OF CREATIVE ACTION

Nothing so bolsters our self-confidence and reconciles us with ourselves as the continuous ability to create; to see things grow and develop under our hand, day in, day out. The decline of handicrafts in modern times is perhaps one of the causes for the rise of frustration and the increased susceptibility of the individual to mass movements.

Eric Hoffer[16]

She's got everything she needs
She's an artist, she don't look back
She's got everything she needs
She's an artist, she don't look back
She can take the dark out of the nighttime
And paint the daytime black

Bob Dylan[17]

My starting point is the psychological fact that the artist has at all times been the instrument and spokesman of the spirit of his age.

Aniela Jaffe[18]

I have no choice. I have to paint.

Anonymous

THE WORK OF ART

The working goal of the artist has always been twofold: the expression of self on the one hand, and expression of the soul of his age on the other. A given piece must be viewed not only from the perspective of the individual but also in the context of the environment from which it emerged. Intentionally or not, the artist brings into creative form the essence of his day, which in its own way has given shape to the artist himself. This is not easy work.

It is no coincidence that the two words *art* and *work* are so often intertwined. We speak of doing artwork. The end products are referred to as works of art. We have spent much time to this point discussing art.

Let us now listen to words related to the definition of work: to put forth effort; to labor and toil; to make way slowly; to affect, influence or provoke; to ferment and seethe; the entire output of an artist.

The working goal of the artist has always been twofold: the expression of self and the expression of the soul of his time.

The Story of Jan

Jan was a beautiful young woman whose good looks and poise helped her attain several modeling jobs early in her professional life. She was bright and pleasant, albeit rather shallow. She complained that although she had a good job and was popular with men, she felt bad all the time and was convinced that her life was futile.

Jan had been raised in a well-to-do family. She said that everything she wanted had always been hers for the asking. To the outside observer she had everything that should have made her happy. Her family loved her, all her material needs were supplied, she had an exciting life . . . and yet Jan had tried to kill herself. That brought her to the hospital and into the art therapy studio.

Her initial collage was on the theme of makeup. She covered a 24″ × 32″ poster board randomly with pictures of lipstick, foundation, blush, eyeliner, eyebrow pencils, mascara and skin conditioner. The pictures, cut or torn from magazine ads, covered nearly every square inch of the board. The effect was nearly overwhelming: cluttered and claustrophobic. Only one small area, about one quarter of an inch in diameter, of white background showed through in one corner of the collage.

Bruce: A lot of makeup . . .
Jan: Yes, it's one thing I do well.
Bruce: Your collage is very full.
Jan: I'd say it's covered up.
Bruce: I'm amazed at how many kinds of makeup you have there.
Jan: Yes, but they are all about the same.
Bruce: There is one little place here that is still white.
Jan: Oh, I didn't realize. Maybe I'd better cover it up.
Bruce: It looks a little overwhelmed.
Jan: Wouldn't you be?
Bruce: Oh, I don't know. It looks clean, too.
Jan: Maybe.

Bruce: If you think of it as clean. I wonder what it's like being
         surrounded by all that makeup.
Jan: It's suffocating.
Bruce: Did you put too much on?
Jan: Maybe, a long time ago.

Jan was in the hospital for several months, but her therapy in the studio seldom moved very far from the theme she introduced in her first work. The art studio became a place where she was expected to put forth effort, make her way slowly, toil, provoke, ferment and seethe as she struggled to remove the emotional makeup she had spent years learning how to apply. The process of working with art was in many ways the first time in her life that things were not handed to her or done for her. She learned to bend wire and form armature structures for sculptures. She skinned her knuckles as she stretched canvas and stapled it to the stretcher. She came to grips in many ways with the possibility that hard work, struggling, was of value in her life. Along with this realization came anger toward her parents, whose depression-era experience made them try to protect their children from the want they had suffered. In the process they had robbed Jan of meaningful opportunities for failure, success, gratification and frustration as she grew up. She was a real, live Barbie doll, endowed with a beautiful facade, burdened with an empty interior.

A few weeks into her hospitalization, Jan began to paint. After several aborted attempts at portraits, still lifes and landscapes, Jan was dejected and frustrated. She asked to have her daily schedule changed so that she could be entered into ceramics and withdrawn from creative arts. Jan and I agreed that she would leave the studio after she had completed one painting. She was irritated by this delay and asked, sarcastically, "What do I have to paint, Boss?" Without responding to her subtle hostility, I suggested she work on the theme of *good-bye.* I told her she could use any style she wanted, but it was important that she finish it.

What emerged as she worked was strikingly different from her other clumsy attempts at mimicking someone else's style or reproducing a photograph in acrylic paint. She began by painting the entire canvas a dark red. She covered the bottom half with black and, leaving a sliver of the intense red, she painted the top portion a deep indigo. The effect was powerful. The red pulsated behind the darker colors, evoking the image of a wound. Here at last was a *work,* not sugar-coated or blemish free; a raw, painful expression of the inner self. The piece screamed for comment, and her fellow patients in the studio responded. Some praised the painting, some patted her on the back. Others looked at it silently before moving on about their own journey.

On the day she signed the work, I asked her if she wanted to talk about it. She said no, she just wanted to stretch another canvas and get to work on her next painting. I went in search of the staple gun.

The entire output of an artist is the sum of his or her willingness and ability to put forth effort, toil and to have patience as the work moves slowly. Further, it is the measure of the artist's tolerance of inner forces that seethe and ferment, soothe and provoke. The work of an artist is not easy or comfortable. It is filled with physical and emotional blisters, scrapes and bruises, strained muscles and scars, cramped fingers and tired eyes.

In this push-button age, the life of the artist remains a story of faith that to struggle with a work in progress is a virtue. Show me a wealthy, overweight, comfortable artist and I'll show you one who has retired.

ART AS LOVE

It often begins in silence. A subtle movement of the soul. An approach, a blush as intentions are made known. A time of gathering. The excitement grows, heart beats quicker. The first touch, tentative. Then more sure, until the grip is strong and tender. The push and pull, motion calling motion, to frenzy. Forces colliding and exploding into color. Dripping and blending, molding and shaping. Hands that pound and hands that caress. Hands that urge and hands that confess, to the silence. And in the stillness I gaze upon the image in the canvas mirror.

Have I described intimacy, or is it a poetic illumination of the artist at work? Perhaps it is both.

The creation of art is an act of love. As the artist draws the first line on the empty paper, the image begins its journey from within to without. "That line then becomes part—the only fixed part—of the image; the rest of the image, as yet unborn, remains fluid."[19]

As the artist adds lines and shapes, the image grows and defines itself. There is a constant ebb and flow of forces between the artist and the emerging image: emotion, imagination, conflict. The creative process is often deeply moving, so filled with nuances of intimacy that it defies precise description. Only the creator can fully experience the depth of the unfolding event. Verbal explanations are awkward, often embarrassing. Janson's metaphor of birth comes closest to capturing the intensity of the process and the event.[19]

The birth metaphor is a stirring one, for it not only acknowledges the joy of the event but calls up the pain, sweat and labor. It transcends the time boundary of a specific moment, in that birth is connected to the long journey through pregnancy, which is connected to a loving act between partners whose love has grown through relationship. Birth is only a point on a time line of relatedness.

I have said that meaning is found in the context of relationships; that is, in transcendence of the self. Creative actions are best appreciated, as well as inspired, in the realm of *community*, which is the shared human experience. Through its approval or rejection, the community confers existential meaning upon the unique expression of the creative act.

Through his work, the artist establishes the context of his love by the accomplishment of his creative strivings. The community is the passive recipient of the fruit of the artist's struggle. With no specific work of its own, with little energy expended, the community receives the product of the creator's personal actualization. It is only in the context of another that the artist can clearly define his unique and separate self. The other comprehends the singularity of the artist. The artist acts out of love as he creates: love for the community and self-love. The community, whether by applause or jeers, acts out their love by taking the art seriously enough to accept or reject. Many artists confirm that the most hateful act of another is indifference to their work.

The mystery of this creative interaction is that love cannot be forced or deserved. Love and creativity are an act of grace. All artists, whether professional or faltering psychiatric patient, know the depth of this mystery. It is sensed when one stands back, surveying the work in progress and knowing . . . *knowing* . . . that this piece will be good. It is felt in the ritual of cleaning brushes for the last time during this painting's creation, knowing that the birthing is over, the child is born. It is heard in the hushed conversations of passers-by as they stop and gaze and grapple with the image. The mystery is there even as the others behold and condemn. Even then the artist/lover experiences a sense of having been addressed.

Love enhances our ability to see value in another and ourselves. For lover and beloved, the world deepens and old details are vested with new worth. "It is well known that love does not make one blind, but seeing. . . . "[20]

Through the mysterious grace of love that enhances all actions and all objects comes the motivation to create again, to be known again, to know again, to love, to create to know. And on the cycle spins.

The story of Tobi

What I knew about Tobi before I met her was that she was 12 years old, depressed and recovering from a very serious overdose of sleeping pills. What no written report could tell me, prior to our first session, was how inadequate the word *depression* can be. Tobi was deeply sad, profoundly sad. She was scared, too, so scared that she quivered as I entered the room. A whimpered moan escaped her tightly closed lips. She looked at me quickly, then averted her eyes. The silence between us roared with windless screams. *Please don't hurt me anymore* seemed to be the message.

Although my manner is naturally gregarious and perhaps a bit too loud, such behavior in Tobi's presence seemed out of the question. The image of a frightened bunny flashed behind my eyes and I sensed that my usual exuberance would be interpreted by Tobi as an attack.

Very quietly I said, "Tobi, my name is Bruce. I understand that you like to draw. I do, too." Saying no more, I went about the task of hanging paper on the wall and taking the chalks out of the cupboard. I taped our papers side by side.

Tobi: Can I go back to my room?
Bruce: You can if that's what you want to do, but . . . "

She went to the door. The attendant was standing outside. I watched them walk back toward the cottage. Tobi looked so frail. I imagined the grey December wind cutting into her.

The next two sessions went much like the first. The fourth time we were scheduled to meet, I had a conflict and was unable to keep our appointment.

The fifth session:

Tobi: Where were you last time?
Bruce: I'm sorry I couldn't be here, Tobi. Something just came up. I tried to call you, but you were at a doctor's appointment. Did they give you the message?
Tobi: Yes, I . . . (long silence).

As I put up the paper, Tobi moved to the cabinet and took out two boxes of chalk.

Bruce: What shall we draw?
Tobi: I want to draw trees.

We drew for about twenty minutes.

Bruce: Feel like talking about the trees, Tobi?
Tobi: No, not now. Would you save it, though?
Bruce: Sure, I'll save it.
Tobi: I think I'd like to go back now.
Bruce: Fine. I think the attendant probably left by now. Can I walk you back?
Tobi: That would be okay.

As we walked through the late afternoon, snow fell quietly around us. Tobi was no louder than the snow. Her coat pulled tightly around her, she seemed to disappear within her woolen shell.

Next session, about ten days before Christmas:

Tobi asked to work on her drawing of trees some more. I unrolled hers and taped it to the wall. The image was of a dense forest. One tree, however, stood out from all the rest. Its roots were exposed above the ground, it had a bluish tint to its trunk and in the middle of the trunk there was a large blackened hollow.

She worked for another half hour, adding more trees to the background, drawing individual leaves and filling in the empty places on the page with myriad tiny details.

When she finished I sat down and began to talk about my tree.

Bruce: This tree stands in the middle of a wheat field. It's been here a long time. There is a woods a long way off on the edge of the field, but for now the tree is by itself.
Tobi: What kind of tree is it?
Bruce: An Oak, I think. My roots go deep into the ground.
Tobi: Why is it so gnarly?
Bruce: The tree has had its share of stormy times. I guess that made it grow funny.
Tobi: It looks lonely.
Bruce: It is, sometimes. But the farmer comes out and eats his lunch there, in the shade. And kids come and play on the low branches.
Tobi: That sounds nice. Mine isn't like that at all.

Bruce: Your forest looks dark.

Tobi: Yeah. It's scary in there.

Tobi spoke for a few moments about how her forest was too thick to walk through. Then she focused on the bluish tree with the gaping hole.

Tobi: Wouldn't this one be pretty if it was in a park?

Bruce: Yes, it's a good tree. It looks strong.

Tobi: It used to be even stronger. Somebody has been taking the dirt away (pointing to where the roots lay above the ground).

Bruce: I wonder why?

Tobi: Me, too.

Bruce: That is a mean thing to do to a tree.

Tobi: Mean things happen in here.

Bruce: That hole in the trunk looks like it might have hurt (no response). Sometimes squirrels build nests in places like that.

Tobi: I don't think anything could live in there.

As I thought about the next session I decided to ask Tobi if she'd be willing to draw a blowup (magnification) of the hole in the tree. She agreed to do so and drew a large black/brown cave-like image. The emotional impact of the drawing was frightening and stark. I asked her if she could pretend to go in there for a while and look around.

Tobi: No, I don't want to.

Bruce: No?

Tobi: I'd be too scared to be in there.

Bruce: I'll go in with you if you want.

Tobi: But it's so dark.

I stood and asked, "Can I draw on your page?" She nodded. I drew a small kerosene lantern with a bright yellow light. "Now we have a light. Draw what you think you might see in this place."

Tobi stood up and added a broken golden ring, a liquor bottle and a ticket to an amusement park. When she finished, tears trickled down her cheeks. "Can we talk next time?" she asked.

I said, "If you want to, but I understand already. . . . It must hurt to look at these things." I stood, with a dark chalk in hand. "Maybe I should turn out the light." I moved as if to draw over the yellow, hoping that she would stop me.

"No," she said, "leave it alone. It's okay to look at that stuff." With that, she went into the next room to wash her hands.

In the weeks and months that followed, light became a recurring metaphor in our sessions together; sometimes in the form of a torch, sometimes a flashlight and occasionally as a harsh spotlight. Tobi, in her quiet and hesitant manner, gradually allowed herself to bring more and more "things to light." Scenes of abuse from an alcoholic father were illuminated. Memories of the battles between her parents prior to and during their separation and divorce were seen. The spotlight lit up the stage on which a tragic drama of disappointment and loss was acted out.

With each session, Tobi was a little more comfortable, a little less frightened. Through her art, she began to allow herself to see and claim feelings and thoughts she had tucked away deep in her own dark forest. As she shared them in the community of two that our sessions composed, she experienced the joy of being understood by another.

When I was very small it was always a wonderful experience to bring my skinned knees to my mother. She would stop what she was doing for a few minutes to sit and hold me on her lap. Regardless of what pain I brought, being held and loved always made things better. I could even survive the peroxide's sting because I knew that sitting on Mom's lap would follow.

My drawings of light and my willingness to understand Tobi were something like that. She felt loved, attended to by one who sought only her growth and betterment.

In our last session together Tobi and I decided to draw each other as animals in a clearing. It's been a long time since then and I can't remember how I symbolized her, but I will never forget the drawing she did of me. I was used to being characterized as some aggressive animal such as a lion or stallion. Tobi drew me as Bambi. As she talked about the drawing she spoke of gentleness and softness. This was the first time a patient had ascribed these attributes to me, and I was deeply moved.

For several years after Tobi left the hospital, I received Christmas cards from her. They always included some kind of lantern in the picture. I had lost touch with her for some time, until this year. At an art therapy conference where I had given a lecture, I was approached by a young woman who asked, "Do you remember me?" Before me stood a grown-up Tobi. She told me that she was in graduate school. I am sure she'll make a fine therapist.

The doing of art is an act of love. The doing of art psychotherapy is also an act of love. Both require great effort. Transcendence of self challenges basic human inertia. To face the challenge and move out for one's own sake or the sake of a patient is an act of courage. The love between therapist and patient is effortful courage.

Therapy, being truly attentive to another, demands bravery and work. It is hard because it hinges on the therapist's willingness to set aside his own desires and biases, to *really listen* to the story being told, and to love.

With these statements, I feel as if I have crawled way out on a tiny limb! It has always intrigued me that presenters at conferences seldom talk about loving. To find references to love in books and articles, one must read between the lines. Will my colleagues misconstrue my meaning when I admit I love my patients? I am sometimes embarrassed among my co-workers to confess that I love my work. So many treaters have followed the path of rational, measurable, scientifically verifiable healing, should I question my own philosophy? Effort is hard to quantify. Bravery defies measuring tools. Love, non-objective, irrational, cannot be submitted for analysis by scientific method.

After years of thinking in negative terms about transference and countertransference, I have come to accept as normal the feelings my patients have for me and I for them. Rather than to attempt to avoid them, I have come to view them as an integral part of the journey. Scott Peck says, "It is essential for the therapist to love a patient for therapy to be successful, and if the therapy does become successful, then the therapeutic relations will become a mutually loving one."[21]

As I stand before the canvas and see what I have done, as I attend to the story my patient/artist tells, I am awed by the work, the courage and the love that I am able to give and receive.

> *In the dime stores and bus stations*
> *People talk of situations*
> *Read books, repeat quotations*
> *Draw conclusions on the wall*
> *Some speak of the future*
> *My love she speaks softly*
> *She knows there's no success like failure*
> *And that failure's no success at all*
>   Bob Dylan[17]

It is so hard to measure what can't be seen.

ART AS LANGUAGE

Drawings, paintings, sculptures, symphonies, poems, dances and dramas are not simply ideas. They are snapshots of life, pieces of reality. Each brushstroke, each chiseled hollow, every harmony, every internal rhyme, all steps and tragedies announce to the world: *I, the artist, was here, and I had something to say. Here it is!*

The gestalt of an artwork is often indescribable in words. Just what did Hopper mean to say in "The Diner"? What exactly was E E cummings trying to tell us in *Anyone Lived in a Pretty How Town?* Such questions can inspire lengthy dialogue or argument, but I am wary of any who claim to know the answer. The configuration of the artist as a biological, social, cultural, familial, internally and externally dynamic creator is over-whelmingly complex. The best that the onlooker can do is catch fleeting glimpses of the multileveled communications of the artist. From these glimpses are formed the first words of the dialogue between creator and audience. When I go to a gallery and stand before a piece, I try first to listen. Faint echoes reverberate across centuries, or decades, or days and I hear the sound of the creator's brush caressing or pummeling the canvas. As the sounds grow louder, I catch a mumbled word or two, perhaps a grunt or a sigh, maybe even a laugh.

In origin, all language is imaginative and expressive of thoughts or emotions. The affective function of language is to express feelings imaginatively. Its cognitive function is to express the intellect imagina-tively. Many before me have written about the distinctions between these two functions of language. The difficulty in discussing these in relation to art and existential art therapy is that the functions are fused within the image. To separate emotion from thought in the context of a piece of art is impossible. The Greek philosophers, those great dividers of mind, body and soul, would no doubt disagree with my insistence that emotion and thought are inseparable when projected onto canvas. I would fur-ther argue that the language of art is comprised not only of cognition and affect but of physical sensation and spirit as well. Attempts to separate these in relation to art are pointless.

As a viewer of art I cannot focus on the expressed thought to the exclusion of the feelings, physical effort and soul of a given piece. To attempt such dissection would be to do gross symbolic violence to the art and the creator. This is true for the fine arts and especially significant in relation to patient artists' work. We must always approach the work of our patients with a sense of awe and reverence for the story they have communicated through their art.

In his novel, *Bluebeard,* Kurt Vonnegut presents a conversation between two writers who might well represent artists of any kind. The focus of the dialogue is why people do their art.[22]

> *"Everybody thinks he or she can be a writer," he said with airy irony.*
> *"Don't tell me it's a crime to try," she said.*
> *"It's a crime to think it's easy," he said. "But if you're really serious, you'll find out quick enough that it's the hardest thing there is."*
> *"Particularly so, if you have absolutely nothing to say," she said. "Don't you think that's the main reason people find it so difficult? If they can write complete sentences and can use a dictionary, isn't that the only reason they find writing hard: they don't know or care about anything?"*

Each time a patient dabs a paint-filled brush to the canvas, each time she scrawls words on scraps of paper, each time his callused fingers dance on the rosewood neck of a guitar, the artist proclaims to the world, *I know something. I care.* As we behold the proclamations, we must gently seek dialogue with their tired muscles, their battered feelings, racing minds and turbulent souls. We must listen to the whole of their communication and at every turn resist the temptation to analyze the affective component in isolation, or the cognitive element, or the sensory traces, or the spiritual glimpse of the artist.

Words Beyond Words

> *A glimpse*
> *a shadowy notion*
> *filling me with smoke*
> *I cough and startle*
> *stutter on the world within*
> *windy, winding, washing over me*
> *lashing out at me*
> *snarling*
> *gnarling around my head like a snake*
> *and I speak these words to you*
> *I'm withered*
> *I'm wilting under your watchful eye*
> *wanting to toss you a glimpse*
> *knowing of course that you'll try to catch it*
> *(running, leaping, diving, arms outstretched)*
> *and come away with elbow scrapes and bruises*
> *coughing from the wisps of smoke*
> *startled*
> *glimpsing*

Cathy Moon

ART AS COMMUNICATION

The Telling of Tales

When I was small and fell and scraped my knee, or if I saw a yellow butterfly, or wondered why robins' eggs are blue, I was always sure that my mother's lap was a safe place to go, to tell my tales and ask my questions. In the magical way of mothers, she always seemed to understand. In the time between then and now I have learned many lessons about the inability of the grown-up world to hold me and understand and answer my questions. And so I have learned to paint, and I teach others to paint as well.

The expression of emotion through art is seldom projected upon any audience. On the contrary, it is an expression from the self to the self. Since nothing can be understood until it has been expressed, the artist is often as surprised by the nature of the feelings as is his audience.

Working in the studio with my patients, I hear a recurring question as I prepare a new canvas: "What are you going to paint?"

My response is generally, "I don't know." This is often misinterpreted as an avoidance of their question. It is the most honest answer I can find. I never know what I am going to paint until I am almost finished with the work. Even when I discipline myself to paint or draw from nature or some life theme, I still, in the deepest sense, do not know why I have chosen a particular subject or how my inner self will direct the execution of the work.

My openness to my own artistic pursuits provides an atmosphere of contagious enthusiasm for self-exploration. This is of vital importance to the existential art therapist. As I paint, sculpt or draw in the presence of the patient, I am keenly aware that my relationship with my art has a critical influence, for good or ill, upon my patient. I tell my tale in the presence of the other, setting the stage for the sharing of stories that is the foundation of the art psychotherapy pilgrimage. Although the communication may sometimes be painful, it is always encouraging to me. The courage that I celebrate as I listen to my art is contagious. It establishes a safe milieu in which patients may also begin their own self-exploration. As they do, their expressions leak, trickle or gush onto the page. If I can be open enough to understand what they have expressed, the patients feel the double edge of pleasure: the clarifying of emotions for themselves and sensing the comprehension of another.

In My House

The House Fantasy is a guided imagery drawing exercise that I use now and again. I believe I created the exercise, although ownership of such things is hard to claim. It is begun with a brief period of relaxation breathing techniques and a few moments of silence. I then tell the group:

I would like you to imagine that you have been asleep for a very long time. You are just beginning to wake up, and you yawn and stretch. As you become more awake you realize that you are in a house you've never been in before. What kind of place is this? Look around you. What do you see? And now you're completely awake and you begin to explore ... get to know this place. . . . As you are walking around you come upon a stairway that seems to lead down into the basement. You're a little hesitant, but finally your curiosity gets the best of you and you decide to go into the basement. As you go down the steps the air gets a little cooler, the light a little dimmer. At the bottom of the steps, at a distance, you see an old stone wall. What else can you find in this basement?

What does it smell like? Run your hands along the walls. How do they feel? And now you find yourself leaning against the stone wall and looking back towards the stairs. Suddenly, one of the stones falls away and you realize that there is another room behind this wall—a secret place. You pull away some more loose stones and more light enters the secret place and you can begin to see what's there. You keep pulling stones away until at last the hole is big enough for you to climb through. Somehow this feels like an important place. Go in, look around ... pick things up, touch them. . . . Know this secret room.

Following the guided imagery trip, each person's paper is divided into three sections. The instruction is to draw (1) the room where you wake up, (2) the basement and (3) the secret room.

Over the past few years I have been a co-therapist in an expressive art psychotherapy group for adolescent boys. The patients referred to this group generally have various sorts of learning disabilities, severe difficulties relating to peers and authorities and great difficulty controlling impulses, particularly when angry. They are typically quite hostile. Beneath the hostility is a perception of themselves as loathesome and inadequate. In the early stages of their participation in the group they tend to be guarded, suspicious and concerned with maintaining a *macho* appearance.

Integration of one such individual into an existing group is often a delicate matter requiring much planning and patience. Not long ago, the group went through a particularly difficult period. There had been three rather abrupt discharges because of insurance denials. For several weeks the group consisted of two patients and the two therapists. Then one of the patients was referred to an auxiliary treatment program, precipitating his departure from the group as well. Thus, a group that usually functions with five or six members and two therapists was reduced to two therapists and one patient. The word quickly spread that there were now several openings in the group and we received four requests for consultation. All of these referrals were appropriate and were admitted. These events occurred just three weeks before my co-therapist, Deb DeBrular, was to go on vacation for two weeks. Our policy was to admit one patient at a time into the group, but I did not want to admit new members while she was gone, nor did I want to make anyone wait a month or more for entry. We decided to admit all four within two weeks. This naturally led to intensification of the resistance patterns. There was no established positive cultural norm within the group and the process deteriorated into devaluing, avoidant, hostile ventilation about anything having to do with therapy. At this point, Deb left for her vacation and I was left with five angry boys.

Into this milieu I brought the House Fantasy. As the guided image portion of the session began, there were giggles and exclamations, such as "What the fuck is he doing?" or "This is stupid to the max." But by the time we were heading down the steps into the basement, there was an air of quiet interest in the room.

For the first time, the boys were attentive as I gave the instructions for the drawing task. When I finished, they each stood up and started on their drawings without hesitation. Our drawings completed, we sat down in the circle and I began by telling my story.

"I woke up in a huge log cabin. It was almost like a mansion but made of logs. There was a thick, dusty, rose-colored carpet on the floor. The thing that really caught my eye, though, in this first room, were big double french doors that led out into a thick woods. It looked like it was spring outside. When I walked down into the basement I was surprised. It seemed like the basement in the house where I grew up. It had a dirt floor and whitewashed walls. But the really neat things in there were the old gravity-type furnace and an antique wooden tool chest. The furnace had a window where one could look in and see the fire. I used to love that furnace when I was little. I'd make up all kinds of stories about it.

The tool chest held some very old tools—a hand saw, a drill, old hammers and screwdrivers.

"Then I found the secret room. When I got inside, I saw a thick burgundy rug. Sitting on the rug was a lighted candle. The light of the candle fell on a photograph of a white Bengal tiger. The walls were lined with bookshelves, almost like a library."

Carl, one of the more vocal of the resistors, spoke, "So what does all that mean?"

Bruce: What?

Carl: You're all the time saying this stuff means something. So what does all that mean?

Bruce: Hmmm. I'm not exactly sure, Carl. I know it makes me a little nervous, but I'm not real clear why.

Carl: Do you still think it has some secret meaning?

Bruce: I'm sure it must mean something, yes.

Carl: Like what? (pause) What do you think that tiger's all about?

Bruce: I'm glad you asked about that, Carl. That's probably the most confusing thing in the drawing for me. Do you have any idea about it?

Carl: Well, I'm not therapeutic, but I think tigers are bad. . . . I mean, they can rip the shit out of you if they want to.

Bruce: You might have something there, Carl. Not that I'd rip anyone, but when you said that I got the image of a tiger pacing. Like there's all this pent-up energy.

Stu: (another patient) I think they're so graceful.

Bruce: Well, no one ever accused me of being graceful.

Carl: But you are powerful here, and you might not like it, but you could rip us if you wanted to.

Bruce: I don't think of myself in that way, but the drawing might be a reminder from myself to myself about the power I do have.

Carl: You have the name tag and the keys, man.

Bruce: That makes it hard for me to see myself through your eyes. Maybe this tiger is a part of me I'm supposed to pay attention to.

Following this discussion of my drawing we moved on to the images of others. My willingness to engage with the tiger in my secret room set the stage for an unusual level of curiosity on the part of each group member as the stories were told.

When it came time to look at Carl's drawing, he explained in some detail that he had been thinking about his image rather than paying much attention to his peers' dialogues. He had also found a cat in his secret room. The cat was chasing a large rat. The room was dark and frightening.

Carl: I didn't want to go in there. It stunk, and I was worried that the cat might get killed somehow. Rats can be really tricky.

Bruce: You like the cat?

Carl: Yeah, it's a good thing.

Bruce: And the rat?

Carl: Rats are evil, man.

Bruce: Carl, you talked a lot about my drawing and what it might mean. That was pretty helpful to me. Can you do the same thing for yourself?

Carl: I don't know. It's too fucking intense. I don't know what's going to happen next.

Bruce: As I look at your drawing, it feels edgy, almost like this is some kind of a war. . . .

Carl: It's a war alright, all the time.

Bruce: Carl, I know that you haven't been real pleased with being in this group, and that's all right. But I hope it can be a place where, for a little while, there can be a truce. Everybody needs a break from the rat race now and again.

Carl: Yeah, well . . . maybe.

The ritual closing in this particular group was to ask each member what he was leaving with. Typical answers were, "a headache," "chalk on my hands," "nothing." On this day, however, Carl said, "I'm not sure. I guess I feel good. I think you guys know what I mean . . . this is embarrassing."

Beneath Carl's embarrassment was a warmth, the sense of acceptance that comes only in those moments when we feel genuinely understood by another. In the months that followed, Carl regularly brought to the group images of horrific emotional events from his past. He learned the grown-up joy of being known by others as he sharpened his skills, both graphic and verbal. By the time he left the hospital, his tough, silent facade had been replaced by a warm, outgoing approach to life. In one of his last drawings, he drew the rat and the cat sleeping quietly on a rug on the basement floor.

ART AS PLAY

Play: to move swiftly, to touch lightly, to flutter and vibrate, contend with and take part. To move freely, especially within prescribed limits... to bring about work and to keep in action....

Webster's New Collegiate Dictionary[23]

Much of what I have spoken of to this point has carried with it an overtone of seriousness, along with an undertone of the awesome power of the arts. Art is, after all, tied to the realities of both inner and outer worlds. It is cathartic, structuring and integrative. My mentor Don Jones often used the term "arting out" to describe the tasks his patients were engaged in. The arts have a way of evoking and intensifying feelings while at the same instant providing a safe, concretized structure for their expression. Most of my work focuses on the deep, raw nature of artistic endeavor.

At this point, however, I want to remind the reader and myself that art can be playful. Surely lurking within us all, along with our monsters, demons and hero selves, there must also be a frolicker whose joy is as genuine and deep as our pain.

Perhaps the playful, fun part of art is best attested to on the refrigerator doors of millions of American households. There really is a ritual of children showing their latest crayon masterpiece to their parents. The glow and sparkle that emerges on little faces as tape is applied and the drawing is hung is seen time and again. This is only the end point of a journey for the child artist who has spent what is for him or her a long time engaged in the activity of art . . . because it is fun.

The same is true for adult artists. Although they are more often aware of the struggle, the work, the pain that emerges in their art, it is the pleasure, the play of the activity itself, that enables the artist to face again and again the burdens of creating.

Art promotes a real, sensational relationship with the environment. The dancer feels her weight through her feet. She feels the smoothness of the floor and the strain of muscle. The guitarist feels the groove of string through callused fingertips and hears the vibration of the strings. The painter smells the oil and turpentine and feels the spongy resistance of tightly stretched canvas caressed by the paint-filled brush. Art pushes the artist to touch the world. There is tremendous therapeutic value in the act of removing one's sensory blinders long enough to really look at how the vase casts its shadow, or to feel the strain of trying to make your first bar chord on an electric guitar, or even in waking up a little sore the morning after your first movement therapy session. In each of these, there is a heightened awareness of self in the world.

There is a magical quality to art that allows the entry into the world of our daily lives of emotions and experiences that are often held in check. Such art, if viewed from critical aesthetic standards, may be good or bad, but goodness or badness has no connection to its playful work. The aim is to enjoy the process. Play activity is a dynamic source of energy for both the individual and society. It is found in every healthy culture. Any civilization that has "outgrown" the need for play is on the brink of extinction, for lack of interest in its own continuation.

Play is difficult for our culture at this time. Major sports are dominated by media and commercial interests, and money seems more important than the joy of the game. Many believe that we are losing touch with the non-material benefits of play. One needs only to spend a summer season watching Little League baseball to see the pressure that is put on the young players. In my brief experience as an assistant coach, I have seen too many incidents of hostility from parents upset by the play of their own child, the actions of the other coach or the "blind" umpire. To be honest, I have felt flashes of my own lust for conquest as my son crosses home plate. Regardless of my (and others') attempts to remind the kids that the important thing is to play and have fun, I believe they receive powerful unspoken cultural messages, something like . . . *but this is more than a game . . . WIN!* As a culture, we exist currently in an era that is not much fun and is hard to play in.

Play Me A Song

Having grown up in the sixties, I was greatly influenced by the music of my time, particularly the Beatles and Bob Dylan, but there were many others as well. I was given my first guitar for Christmas in 1964. That gift began a love affair with music that lives on today.

Once I learned to play, I set about forming rock 'n' roll groups. There were The Blokes, Galaxy and B. T. Noah, and several more whose names I have forgotten. We played at sock hops, dances and wedding receptions. It was all great fun and a wonderful diversion from the routines of high school. More times than not we played for free, and the gigs were always so far apart that it never felt like work. Always it was a pleasure.

After college, I ran out of time for bands. My musician friends went their separate ways and for a decade or more I played for myself, in the solitude of my room. This was a pleasure of a different kind. My guitar was company when I was lonely. I could always take comfort in my skills when my competencies in other arenas were only beginning to develop. The guitar was a vehicle on which to ride out sorrows and transmit joys.

As often happens with dormant and unresolved potentials, my interest in performing publicly re-emerged. Serendipitously, in 1984 a friend and I were asked to play background music at a social function sponsored by the hospital. This further fueled the fires of old fantasies of professional musicianship. My friend John Reece and I found spare hours in which to practice and in a few months we were ready to begin approaching local clubs with our demo tape. We had some minor successes relatively quickly. For months we played weekend engagements once or twice a month. The novelty, along with the extra money we made, was a pleasant diversion from our "real-life routines."

Late one Saturday night, somewhere around one o'clock in the morning, my fingers ached and my throat was sore. A woman approached us and told us she had enjoyed the music. It hit me at that moment that I had not. In fact, I had hated it. There was no joy in the playing. It had become monotonous, hard work. Soon after that John and I decided it was time to quit. Now we play for fun, every now and then.

The folk singer, Joni Mitchell, has apparently struggled with similar issues. In her ballad, "Real Good For Free," she paints a portrait of a street musician who plays beautifully for free. This is contrasted with her critical self-reflection:

> *I play if you have the money*
> *or if you're a friend to me.*[24]

A similar phenomenon is seen at the Columbus College of Art and Design, where I instruct. Students often grapple with a sense of lost joy as they conform to the school's demand for production. This is, of course, a temporary situation and may in fact be quite valuable as they learn to discipline their creative impulses. Still, it is my hope that after graduation, when all the assignments and problems are complete, they will once again discover the play of doing art.

Playing with Art

Most people who do not describe themselves as artists have an opportunity to experience the playfulness of art. Since art is not generally

considered a likely avenue for professional development, it is less con-
taminated by competitive and materialistic forces. Many of my patients
begin our relationship with the disclaimer, "I am not an artist" or "I
haven't drawn since I was a kid." While some might interpret these
comments as evidence of low self-esteem or inhibition, I prefer to view
them as statements of opportunity. What the patients have shared may
well be that they have no preconceived or rigid notions about their
artistic skills, or that they view art as something children do. In either
case they have identified themselves with the position of the child who is
as yet unskilled, and primarily interested in the pleasure of play. This is
a marvelous place to begin the art therapy journey.

Play It Again, Bill

I was Bill's therapist in both the Creative Arts studio and in Expressive
Art Therapy. In both areas, but in strikingly different ways, Bill rediscovered himself through art.

Bill was a successful workaholic business executive, a conscientious
father and a loyal husband. In many ways he symbolized the American
dream. He had started out as a laborer in the same business of which he
was now vice-president.

Bill was admitted to Harding Hospital after several months of de-
teriorating functioning at work and at home. He complained that he
could no longer concentrate and nothing was enjoyable anymore. A
handsome man in his late thirties, he was well-educated, thoughtful
and polite. There was a disturbing quality about him, however. His
face seemed to sag as if pulled downward by some invisible burden,
and his eyes had a vacant, defeated look. He also had a slight trembling
of his hands. His back bent slightly and his voice sounded tired. He was
a very sad man.

Bill was referred first to the Creative Arts studio, and after a few weeks
he was also assigned to Expressive Art Therapy. His experience in these
two areas illustrate the differences in their possibilities for helping an
individual.

From the Studio:

As I explained the initial tasks to Bill, he passively accepted all
instructions and proceeded to create a collage on the theme of sporting
events. He methodically searched for images in magazines; cutting,
arranging and gluing in a robot-like manner. I watched him work with

an uneasy sensation that for several moments was unnerving. While I worked on my own painting, hearing his movements, sensing his presence in the room, it came to me that his manner reminded me of the walking corpses I had seen in advertisements for the movie, *Night of the Living Dead.* Although Bill was pleasant enough to be with and certainly not gruesome, there was a haunting, lifeless quality to him as he worked.

When he finished his collage on the third day, he stiffly brought it to me for my comments, suggestions or approval. His images were an exhaustive assortment of precisely trimmed pictures of:

> football fields
> basketball courts
> baseball diamonds
> jai lai courts
> infields and outfields
> race tracks
> soccer fields
> tennis courts
> end zones
> penalty boxes
> roller rinks
> racquetball courts
> field hockey fields
> equestrian jump courses
> volley ball courts
> ice rinks
> swimming pools

There were no people in the pictures. The fields and courts were empty, devoid of the action they were designed to contain. The visual effect of such vacancy was stunning. I commented that his collage was very interesting.

Bill: You can have it.
Bruce: Oh, I couldn't do that, Bill. You've worked quite a while . . . but I appreciate your offer. It is an intriguing piece.
Bill: So what should I do with it?
Bruce: Why don't you take it back to the unit, Bill . . . maybe show it to your doctor?
Bill: Okay. What's next?

Later, after all the patients had left the area and I was cleaning up, I noticed Bill's collage, wadded up and thrown in the garbage can. I took it out of the trash, smoothed it as best I could and taped it to the door of the studio. When Bill entered the following afternoon, I watched as a hesitant smile formed, then quickly receded as he stood facing the collage. He immediately reverted to his inhibited, lackluster style of interaction, but I knew that my effort to connect had been acknowledged.

Bill moved on to other creative tasks with a variety of media. In each case, his approach was mechanical, meticulous and stark. Several months went by with him plodding joylessly from project to project. My observations of Bill were consistent with the information I gathered about him from the other members of the psychiatric team. The social worker's assessment was that Bill's marriage was dysfunctional. She described it as dull and utilitarian. Bill's psychiatrist spoke of the flatness of his affect and his lethargy on the unit. The nursing staff expressed concern that Bill isolated in his room during all unstructured hours. My colleagues in Adjunctive Therapy commented on his "just going through the motions."

Bill described the passage of time as being like a rubber band: "Every day stretches out and feels like a week. Every hour feels like a day." And so his time stretched out before him.

The image of Bill's first collage so clearly symbolized his inability to enjoy things, yet the potential was also obviously there. In team meetings there was much pessimism expressed by several team members about Bill's prognosis. They asserted that there had been no glimmer of anything other than his anhedonia in all the months he'd been in treatment. I reminded the team of the collage with its uninhabited playing fields. I suggested that the fields were waiting to be used and that I believed that Bill had the potential for playing, and enjoying life.

One afternoon in December I was working on a chalk drawing of the logo of the Greyhound Bus Company. This was to be used as the background for a Christmas drama that the Adjunctive Therapy staff were staging. Bill entered the studio, looked at my drawing and chuckled. Somehow the sight of me with my face and hands covered with chalk dust before the large (ten feet by four feet) drawing of the greyhound had struck Bill's funnybone. He asked me what I was doing the drawing for and I explained that it was to be used as scenery for a play in which people find themselves stranded in a bus station on Christmas Eve.

Bill: Can I help?

Bruce: Sure. Grab some orange chalk and fill in this section.

We worked for an hour or so finishing up the drawing. In the midst of this work, Bill experimented with techniques of shading and blending the chalk. Although I outwardly kept my focus on the task at hand, I paid close attention to the obvious pleasure this dusty, smeary, colorful medium gave him.

Over the next few weeks I engaged Bill in a variety of artistic exercises using pastel chalk and crayons. He loved the mess he made on his clothes, his face and hands and in the work area. During one session he suggested that he try using the chalk on a gessoed masonite panel. I told him I had never tried that combination, but that he was free to experiment. Experiment he did. He developed a technique of combining chalk, crayon and craypas with layers of varnish on the gessoed masonite. His drawings typically started with a solid color chalk background. Then he made a single gesture line with a contrasting color. This was the foundation from which he worked. A layer of polyurethane was then sprayed on. He then would begin a series of overlays, embellishments and details. Although he worked meticulously, the visual effect was spontaneous and lively.

In Expressive Art Therapy:

Bill had been in the Creative Arts studio only a few weeks when he was assigned to Expressive Art Therapy. When he entered the group room he moved very slowly. After he had been introduced to the others in the group, I asked him if he had ever tried to draw his feelings before.

Bill: No, I haven't drawn anything since I got too old for crayons.

Bruce: Well, this will be something really different for you then.

Bill: I don't know why they put me in this group. It sounds a little useless to me.

Bruce: That's one way to look at it.

Bill: What do we do, anyway?

Bruce: Usually we draw about feelings. When we're done we throw them away.

He looked a bit surprised by this and asked, gruffly, "What do you mean, you just throw them away? We don't get to keep them or anything?"

Bruce: Well, you can keep your drawings if you want to, but that isn't the point.

Some of the other group members chimed in that sometimes it felt really good to crumple up the things they drew and trash them.

Bruce: For our warm-up drawing today, I'd like you all to divide your page into four sections. Label one section *Happy,* one *Sad,* one *Angry* and one *Love.* Now, what I'd like you to do is to use colors and lines or shapes to fill in each section with colors that express those feelings for you.

Bill began to draw a smiley face in his *Happy* section. I quickly intervened.

Bruce: No, Bill, no drawings of things allowed here. Just use lines or colors.

Bill: You mean it shouldn't look like anything?

Bruce: That's right.

Bill began to draw again but this time used very light and sparse markings. He was working on the *Angry* section.

Bruce: C'mon, Bill, you can fill the box with colors. Don't be so shy.

At this comment, he irritably picked up a red chalk and slammed it against the paper.

Bruce: Good, that's more like it.

When everyone had finished drawing, we went around the circle and looked at each person's images. Bill's face brightened noticeably when he saw all the similarities between his graphics and those of his peers. All of the angry drawings contained red and black slashing lines. The sad segments each had blue as a dominant color. All the happy drawings utilized yellow. There was a great variety in the images themselves, but enough similarity to stimulate discussion about the language of art that is a part of all human beings, whether they have art training or not. Everyone knows about singing the blues, or seeing red, or feeling sunny or being green with envy. These cliches are born of deep psychological responses to color. The same is true of line character. If you ask someone to imagine a chalkboard and make an angry line, invariably the fist will clench and move in harsh, angular, jerking motions. Line and color are the foundations of two-dimensional visual art. All persons have the groundwork to express themselves artistically.

Bruce: For our main drawing today I'd like us to use this same process of colors and lines to fill the whole page with the feeling you have most often.

Bill sat, sagging in his chair.

Bill: I just don't know.

Bruce: Okay, Bill, what is your favorite color?

Bill: Orange.

Bruce: Well, what I want you to imagine, since orange is your favorite color, is that it represents all the good feelings in life, like love and happiness and fun.

Bill: What do you want me to do?

Bruce: Let's work together. And since you're going to use orange, I think I'll use blue. Blue is the opposite of orange, you know. And let's say that blue represents all the bad feelings, like guilt and sadness and hopelessness.

Bill: (sighing) Whatever you say.

The paper Bill was to work on was approximately three feet by four feet in size and taped to the wall.

Bruce: What we're going to do is have a race. I'm going to divide the page in half. You work on one side and I'll work on the other. Let's think of it this way: you have about thirty more years to live, on the average, and so we'll divide them evenly, fifteen years of bad feelings and fifteen years of good. That seems only fair. . . .

With that, I began to fill up my side of the paper. Bill stood beside me, befuddled. I turned to him.

Bruce: Well come on, Bill. You're making it easy.

He began tentatively to scratch his chalk on the page. Since I'd worked quickly, I ran out of room on my side.

Bruce: Well, my side is all full. Tell you what, Bill, I'm going to take another five years of your happy side, okay?

I began to draw on his side of the page. Bill stopped drawing momentarily and looked at me incredulously. I finished my extra five years section and turned to him.

Bruce: Well, it's obvious that you don't mind this, so I think I'll take another five years off your side. That leaves you with. . . . hmmm. . . . only five years out of the next thirty. That will be good. Oh, well, that's the way it goes sometimes.

I began to draw my blue over his orange marks.

Bill: That's about enough!

He raised his voice. I pretended not to hear him. He shouted.

Bill: I said that's about enough!
Bruce: Show me, Bill.

By this time I had covered nearly the entire page with blue. Bill slammed his orange against the wall, pushed my arm out of the way and aggressively attacked the blue with his orange. I pushed back, and for a couple of minutes we wrestled back and forth on the page. There were grunts and groans. Both of us worked up a good sweat as chalk dust filled the air. At some point, Bill began to laugh. By the time we finished, we both looked as if we had just emerged from a coal mine. The other group members applauded and Bill continued to chuckle as they praised his orange triumph.

At first look, this vignette might be confusing. Some may want to focus on the evocation of pent-up anger that occurred. While this certainly happened for Bill, I believe it was the sensuousness of the pushing and pulling, the sweating and silliness of it all, that for a period of time broke through the weighted, ponderous approach to life that Bill had assumed. This was not a magical cure, by any means, but it was the first step in Bill's reclamation of the ability to play. At the end of the session, as the attendant walked with him out the door, I overheard:

Attendant: You look like you've been in a war.
Bill: I was, and it was fun.

In the months that followed in the hospital, Bill rediscovered long forgotten or abandoned skills on the ping-pong table, the volleyball court, the piano and in the art studio. He has developed into an accomplished watercolorist and has learned to balance his life's work with his life's play.

Of course, while Bill was developing his playful style in the art studio, honing his ping-pong skills and struggling to give form and image to his feelings in the group room, equally significant work was proceeding with his psychotherapist and other staff members. All pieces of the therapeutic puzzle are interdependent and each is enhanced by the others. Still, it was in Bill's art that we first glimpsed the possibilities. It was in his first collage that I sensed that he might someday be able to *play* again.

ART AS PRAYER

In June of 1988, Ursuline College in Cleveland, Ohio, hosted a conference titled, "Spirituality and the Arts." In the course of one of the discussions after a presentation, my friend and colleague Deb DeBrular commented that for her doing art was much like praying. My wife and colleague, Cathy Moon, stirred in her seat. She whispered excitedly to her close friend Deb, "I can't believe we have never talked about this aspect of our work. That's the way it is for me, too. I've often thought of art as praying. In fact, that's what I wrote about in my paper."

Despite having spent several years studying in a Methodist seminary, I had never thought of art in that way. I suppose it is possible to be too close to something to be able to see it. Since the Ursuline conference I have been intrigued by the notion that as I paint, I pray.

A dictionary definition of prayer is "to offer adoration, confession, supplication and thanksgiving to God." Adoration, confession and thanksgiving are relatively easy aspects of both prayer and painting for me to grasp. The concept of supplication, however, was difficult to relate to. For a while I shelved the attempt. It was not until I happened to be looking through some photographs of my old paintings that the idea of painting as a humble petition became clear.

The painting (Fig. 4) was done in 1978, soon after Cathy and I learned that she was pregnant with our first child. There are so many elements to this piece, it is difficult to summarize. Briefly, the themes are: a cloudy portrait of the ghost of my father standing outside a Veterans of Foreign Wars hall, looking quietly in my direction; a representation of me, looking away and slightly to the left side of the canvas; my wife at the lower left, sitting on the bed where this child had been conceived; a still life of grapes, a bottle of wine and a lighted hurricane lamp. Above this is a segment of a soiled American flag, and finally above this is a landscape. On the lower right there is a section of seascape.

This painting has been a mystery for me ever since the day I signed it. It has always been one of my favorite works without my really knowing why. On the afternoon I leafed through the photographs of paintings, it at last began to make sense to me. It is, I believe, a prayer of supplication.

I have mentioned earlier that my father died when I was a baby and I have no memory of him at all. Still, this man who was my father, of whom I have heard glorious and frightening stories, who was wounded in

Figure 4. "As I approached the reality of fatherhood I was deeply frightened."

World War II, who drank too much, who really knew Dizzy Dean and who was the only man my mother ever loved, has had an incredible impact upon my life through his absence. As I approached the reality of fatherhood I was deeply frightened. What did I know about being a dad, anyway? What if I did it all wrong? And what would this do to my relationship with Cathy? What if something goes wrong? What if something happens in birth, or to me? And what if . . . on the questions went.

There was also a deep empty place in me that shouted in celebration. At last I would find out what a real father-son relationship is like.

Looking at this painting now, I hear a humble petition, "God, help me." The painting united all the parts of me as I approached fatherhood: the sea with its depth and awesome vastness; the ghost of my father who was never there, but always there; my beautiful wife, partner who was brave enough to face these things with me; the image of wine, a symbol of life; the light in the darkness; and finally the tree, which grows strong and solid from the earth, ever deepening and widening its roots. All these elements combine in the simple visual prayer, *God, help me be a good enough father to this unborn child. Amen.*

Regardless of the form one's faith takes—faith in God, or gods, or life itself—it is reflected in the art we make. As an existential art therapist I regard the journey as a sacred quest that my patients and I engage in. Since the primary mode of our communication is the images we create, they are the visual prayers of the pilgrimage. In the cloister of our studio, confessions are uttered, thanksgivings shared and praises sung. It is a holy thing we do, this making art and healing wounds.

The Story of John in the Wilderness

John entered Harding Hospital after several bouts of chest pains and trips to the emergency room, where each time he was examined and pronounced to be in perfect physical health. John was convinced that all the doctors were wrong and that he would soon die.

John was a protestant minister who, like many in his profession, attempted always to meet the needs of everyone around him. He had been promoted steadily within his denomination; first serving a small rural two-church charge, then a modest suburban church and finally a large urban congregation. With each move, the demands on his time and energy increased. This caused tension with his wife and distance from his family, which inhibited his performance at work, which made him want to work even harder, which distanced him more than ever from his wife. On and on the binding cycle went. As his relationships and performance deteriorated, his bishop applied pressure, which only heightened the difficulties. John sought solace in a relationship with an attractive church secretary. It eventuated in an affair that left him feeling guilty, isolated and bound.

On his first day in the group, John responded to the theme, "draw yourself where you are" by creating an image of himself as John the Baptist standing in the wilderness. The problem, he said, was that he had forgotten just what it was he was supposed to proclaim. I asked John how it felt to be out there all alone. He talked about theology and the scriptural reference but could not identify any feelings at all in the drawing. John truly was lost. Desperately out of touch with his feelings, his needs, he was alone in a wilderness all his own.

I began the next session by telling the following story, *The Innovator* by G. William Jones.

* * * * *

Confession is Good for the Cell

Amos was dragged to the prison kicking and screaming.

"But I'm innocent, I tell you!" he shouted for the seven-hundred and fifty-fifth time as the turnkey slammed his cell door.

"Yeah, we're all innocent, buddy," came the harsh voice of Amos's next cell neighbor. "I been here on a bum rap for fifteen years now—as innocent as the warden though I am—maybe innocenter!"

After a few weeks of screaming himself hoarse about his innocence, Amos finally settled down to a routine that divided equal time between brooding over the injustice of it all and making feverish plans for getting the truth of his innocence before the right people. He spent many hours daydreaming of the governor's embarrassment when he hand-delivered the pardon to Amos's cell. The governor would sputter and fumble and blush in an agony of self-reproach over imprisoning such a noble, innocent man, while Amos would keep a stern and unreadable face. The governor would offer all kinds of enticements to mollify Amos—new cars, a fine suburban home with swimming pool and pool table, a setup into his own little business—but no, Amos would sue. His revenge would be as monumental as the injustice they had wreaked upon him. Amos's little eyes glittered in the gloom of his cell as he drank in the mental picture of the day when his innocence would triumph.

In the meantime, Amos did what he could on the home front. When he wasn't writing ten-page letters to senators and congressmen, he was at his post at his cell door shouting his innocence to everyone who passed by. When he didn't receive replies from most of his letters, he accused the warden of tampering with federal mails. He shouted that too.

One day, when Amos had been locked up in his cell for almost a year, his eyes became tired from following the long letter he was writing with a stubby pencil. To rest his eyes, he went to his cell window and looked out and down to the courtyard. The sight of grass greening and buds popping shocked him!

Somehow he had forgotten that there was an outside, or at least that life, time and the world were still going on beyond his bars. Because his own life had been stopped in mid-beat by his imprisonment, he had let himself imagine that the whole world had stopped, too—as if waiting with caught breath for that glorious day of the triumph of Amos's innocence, that day when he would emerge from the hated prison.

It was too much for Amos—the grass, the buds, everything living and growing and changing but him. He was trapped. It wasn't the world that hung in suspended animation while Amos busily scribbled and shouted; it was Amos who was trapped, immobile, like a bee in amber, while the rest of the world seethed by and around him. With a gasp Amos swept the carefully lettered pages from his bunk and fell groaning into it.

It was dark in the cell by the time that supper came.

"Here you go, Mr. Innocent," the turnkey joked as he slid Amos's tray through the slot in the iron door.

"I'm not innocent," Amos croaked, weary with it all. "I'm guilty. Guilty as hell."

"What did you say?" the turnkey asked, strangely excited, holding his breath to catch the soft answer.

"Guilty," sighed Amos. "I'm guilty."

Immediately there was a rattling of the key in the lock, and when Amos raised his head the door didn't look right. When he got up and gave the door a tentative push, it swung open broadly into the dusky, deserted corridor.

Peeping timidly down the corridor, Amos saw that other gates were hanging open before him all the way to the front gate. There was still enough sunlight left to give him a glimpse of the greening grass and the bursting buds beyond.[25]

* * * * *

As I finished the story I saw two tears trickling down John's face. I asked the group to draw their responses to the parable. John drew himself sitting on the steps in the front of his church's sanctuary, leaning against the base of the pulpit. Sitting in the pews were his wife and children, his secretary, his bishop and members of all the congregations he had served. When I asked him to share what he could with the group about this image, he said, "I think I need to tell them . . . and me . . . who I am, what I really think and feel."

John remained in the hospital for a little over a month. He nicknamed the expressive art group his "confessional." It is of note that no one in the group other than John and I knew about his affair or any of the other historical facts that led up to his admission to Harding. What they did know about John was that he was a man who sometimes felt scared and angry, lustful, happy and needy. In this way they learned who John really was, and John was able to come in from the wilderness.

Lisa Remembers How to Give

Lisa had been in the expressive group therapy for several weeks. She had come to Harding Hospital after several failed attempts at outpatient therapy and short-term hospitalization. She had manifested a variety of self-destructive and self-defeating behaviors. Alcohol and drug abuse, promiscuity, stealing and suicidal gestures had become the habits of her existence.

In the group she was rude to her peers, hostile towards my co-therapist and me, and generally disruptive and devaluing of the group and treatment. One day, quite by chance, as we were walking through the hallway back to the living unit, we happened upon Lisa's younger brother and sister. They had come for a family visit. Lisa had not seen any of her family for several weeks. When she saw these two small children, ages four and five, she burst into tears and ran to them, picked them up and hugged them. What a contrast to the angry young woman I had been working with! When Lisa talked in the group about her family, she was always bitter and enraged towards her parents. This display of warmth and tenderness was a ray of hope in what had been a bleak landscape.

Up to that time we had focused Lisa's therapy on exploration of her feelings of abandonment and self-loathing. While these were clearly the issues of her pathology, the interaction with her siblings did offer a slightly different direction in which to go. It reminded us of Viktor Frankl's insistence that meaning in life can only be found in self-transcendence. At the next group session I instructed all members of the group to put their name at the top of their page, then move to the person's paper on their right. When everyone had done so, I said, "It is often easy for us to forget what we have to offer to other people. This is particularly true when we are feeling bad. Today I want us to remember to think about the person whose page you are facing, and draw a gift for that person. You have the power to give anything you think they need. When you are done, move to the next person's page, and keep going until you are back at your own paper."

Lisa, who had so often been caustic and disruptive, proceeded to draw intensely. To one peer she gave a home "where people love you." To another she gave a shoulder to cry on. To another she gave a megaphone so she could speak up for herself. To my co-therapist she gave a door that stood slightly open. To me she offered a scene at the beach, a peaceful place. Lisa's verbal explanations of her gifts were sensitive and eloquent. The atmosphere of the group room, so often the site of battles, was warm and caring.

When all of us had shared our drawings with one another, I stated my belief that all things we create are a self-portrait. Lisa quietly looked again at the things she had drawn. "No, that can't be me. I'm rotten and dead," she said.

I replied, "Lisa, I believe you. I know there are parts of you that feel horrible, but I see the other parts, too. I've watched you hold your little sister, and I've just now seen the gifts you have to offer people here."

In the months that followed this session, Lisa gradually became more accepting of her good self-potentials through her relationships with others. Simultaneously she learned to be gentle and loving with her ugly, ruined and broken parts of her self as well. Her images moved from blackened smoldering garbage heaps to fragile wild flowers. Stereotypical slogans like "fuck the world" and "anarchy" were abandoned as she embraced the whole of herself.

Lisa's last graphic image was a union of opposites. She portrayed a devil figure and a saint in white playing tug of war. Woven into the strands of the rope were the words *thank you.*

In spite of the years I've spent in theological study, or perhaps because of it, I find myself still unsure of what lies beyond the realm of human experience. There have been times I've thought of myself as an agnostic, and at times I've believed myself to be a Christian. Regardless of which position I'm in, thanks to Cathy and Deb, I regard my art and that of others as prayer. Whether prayers to God, or the gods, or life itself does not trouble me, for it is the praying that recalls that element of self-transcendence which is the basis of the sacred task of healing.

ART AS MASTERY

The Elephant and his Man: a Parable

A man had wandered the countryside for many months, looking for the meaning of it. Along the way he had met others from all walks of life, and since the land was a magical place he had even encountered the likes of a talking cactus and a rock that could dance.

On this day, as he walked through a forest, he began to hear a strange trumpeting sound in the distance. As he got closer to the source of the noise, he could feel the earth tremble now and again. At last his path led into a clearing, and there standing on the bank of a stream stood a huge grey elephant. Beside the beast was a slim brown-skinned man. The wanderer watched as the small man raised his hand. At this signal the elephant reared back and balanced on its two hind legs, raised its trunk and blasted its trumpet call. It then fell forward with such a force that the ground shook as its front feet pounded the bank.

The wanderer was enthralled with the scene. He thought to himself, "Oh, to be the master of such an animal! What power this is! Surely this man will know the meaning of it." And so the pilgrim approached the elephant and its master. He introduced himself and explained his quest to the man. Having done so, he asked, "Will you tell me, sir, what is the meaning of it?"

The man patted his elephant and chuckled, "Why in the world do you ask me?"

The pilgrim replied, "Because it is so clear that you must have great knowledge and power in order to so control this massive beast."

The master's chuckles turned to boisterous laughing. Amid his spasms he said, "You think I control him?" and he guffawed all the more.

"Of course I do. I've seen you. You raise your hand and the animal rises on two legs. . . . "

The master composed himself and again caressed the leather-hard skin of the elephant. "Excuse me for laughing so. I don't mean to be rude. It's just the thought that I control him is rather astounding."

Perplexed, the pilgrim asked, "But surely you are the master, are you not?"

The small brown man sighed. "I suppose I am a master, but not the kind you describe. What you see my big friend do when I raise my hand is nothing more than a gift he offers me."

"What are you saying?"

"I am a master, it is true. I am the master of carrying hay and leaves for him to eat. I am the master of scrubbing his hide and cleaning him. I am the master of hauling water when we are in a dry place. I am the master of shooing flies away from his eyes, and I am the master of talking to him in the midst of his isolation from his fellow beasts. All these things I do to the best of my abilities. I have practiced these tasks for years and I believe I do them well."

"But the elephant does what you tell him to."

"No, no. He is always free to do what he pleases. How could I stop him? It is a gift, his way of thanking me perhaps for my masterful feeding and bathing."

Patients beginning their art psychotherapy pilgrimage often feel much like the wanderer in the parable, wondering what is the meaning of it, and relating to the mastery part of the story. For many, admission to the hospital is a dramatic symbol of their brokenness. Lamentations, such as, "I am useless," "Nothing matters," "I'm a pain in the ass," and "Life sucks," are not uncommon. Such negative self-evaluations often mark the landscape in the early miles of the journey.

It is fascinating to encounter the illogic of self-depreciation. Consider, for instance, the case of a young woman who had completed a master's degree in chemistry. She was a skilled athlete, a devoted friend, beloved daughter. Still, she bombarded herself with hostile epithets. To others she was the picture of competence, intelligence and success; yet to herself she was loathsome. She found no meaning, no sense of lasting value in her competencies.

The arts provide an experience in mastery that goes much deeper than skill and intellect. This can be illustrated by comparing the lasting values of technology and art. For instance, by the year 1955, television was well-established as a technological success. In the year 1989, however, no one wants to watch programming on a 1955 black-and-white TV. Technology has passed it by, and although there may be some 1955s still around as collector's items, they are curiosities. What was once the state of the art is now obsolete and valueless. Contrast this with the art of Jackson Pollack, whose paintings attract the same intense attention and controversy that they did in 1955. Further, they have increased in monetary value. The value of art is deeper and more lasting because it draws directly from primordial potential. The development of artistic expression and skill binds the artist to all of creative human history.

The Story of Tori

Tori was a shy and introverted girl. Although intelligence tests showed her to have an average I.Q., she had never done well in school. She was socially immature and if given the choice, she preferred to stay alone in her room rather than join the world around her. She had an air of fragility that kept people at a distance. No one wanted to hurt her.

When Tori entered the Creative Arts studio she made an unusual request. In a hestitant and quivering voice she said, "I want to learn to draw glass."

"Glass?" I asked.

"Glass," she said.

So we embarked upon an artistic pilgrimage of mastering techniques of drawing glass. We began with the basic shapes: circles, squares, rectangles, cones, triangles. As might be expected, Tori's inhibited approach to the world was symbolized by her timid engagement with the page. Her first drawings, which she chose to do with very hard lead pencils, were small and so lightly drawn as to be nearly invisible from any distance. After several sessions of these tight and constricted images, I introduced a new medium. I had found some old poster chalks, about one inch in diameter and three or four inches long. I taped several large sheets (3 feet square) of brown wrapping paper to the wall and told her again that I wanted her to draw the basic shapes. I added that each shape must be about the size of a record album.

She sighed, "This is going to be really hard."

"Yes, I know it will, but I believe you can do it, Tori."

She spent three or four sessions getting used to the thick black chalk. By this time Tori had been working in the studio for about two weeks. She would occasionally ask quietly what drawing shapes had to do with drawing glass. My response was that people learn first to roll over, then crawl, then walk, then run. "We're learning to roll right now."

Tori became increasingly adept at drawing shapes. She was more careful and less skittish with her lines. She was able to press firmly on the paper and move with some level of assuredness. The next phase of her learning related to line quality.

"This week, Tori, you are going to do nothing but draw straight lines."

"Are you kidding?"

"No, Tori, I'm not kidding at all."

Tori drew lines for the next four sessions. She learned to alter the thickness of the line by varying her pressure on the chalk. She learned to barely touch the paper with her chalk in order to create a razor-thin line. She drew them, and drew, and drew again.

The following Monday I took a volleyball to the studio and set it on a table in front of a large window. The day was bright, so the side of the ball toward the window was brilliant white. The side away from the light cast a strong shadow.

"Tori, today I want you to draw the outline of the volleyball."

She quickly drew a circle.

"C'mon, Tori, this line you drew is the same all the way around. Is that how you see it?"

"What do you mean?"

"I mean, as you look at the ball, what do you see? Is the edge the same all the way around?"

"Oh, I get it . . . like the lines last week?"

She drew the ball again, using a very thin, lightly drawn line where the sun hit the ball. The other side was dark and heavy. Light and shadow could be seen in the character of the line. I suggested she switch back to the #2 pencil and draw the ball once more. When she finished, she smiled,

"I did it right, didn't I?"

"You sure did, Tori."

We progressed from shapes to lines, to shading and finally to a glass of water. At each step Tori's confidence grew. Her manner was less fragile as she interpreted these fundamental skills.

When she confronted the glass, however, she abandoned all the techniques she had acquired. She was so concerned with making it look the way she wanted it to that she forgot to use what she knew. Tori became very frightened, crumpled her paper and tossed it into the wastebasket.

"Tori, what have you done?"

"I threw my drawing of the glass away."

"Ah, that must have been the problem."

"What?" she snapped.

"You said, your drawing of the glass. You were supposed to be drawing the shapes, lines and shadows, not the glass of water. Here, try it again."

Her second attempt, while rough and awkward, was a great improvement over her first work.

Tori drew that glass for many sessions. She drew it in pencil, with pen and ink, with chalk, with charcoal, with craypas and crayon. She became the master of that glass. She knew it backwards, forwards, upside down and right side up. After a time she moved on to other glass objects, bottles and vases, mirrors and cups. She stayed with a subject long enough to render it well and then moved on. All the while she became more spontaneous in the studio, louder and more self-assured.

I make no claim that her mastery of drawing glass alone empowered her to move out of her fragile style. I do believe that it symbolized clearly for her the heart of her therapy. She had entered the hospital afraid and out of control of herself in the world. When she left she was the master of her own fragility.

Near the end of her stay, I took H. W. Janson's *History of Art* with me to the studio. Tori flipped through the pages, occasionally pausing at a color plate or black-and-white photo. She particularly liked Edouard Manet's *A Bar at the Folies Bergere*.

"He handled the glass very nicely."

Chapter X

THE ARTIST ON THE CUTTING EDGE

As an existential art therapist I believe that everything we create is a self-portrait. Not that any single painting or song or dance is the complete piece; rather, that each creative act is a facet of a continuously evolving prismatic portrait of the creator. Looking back over twenty years' worth of my paintings, I glimpse the growing sum of who I am. This is a little like gazing into a mirror in a dimly lit room. Each new creation slightly brightens the light and I see a bit more clearly. Looking into the mirror is sometimes pleasant, sometimes disturbing. Some days I like what I see; some days I want to hide my eyes.

Writing papers, or a book, is a creative act, much like painting and songmaking. These too provide glimpses of my portrait. The focus of this chapter is cultural imagery, the good and the evil I see around me and the impact these images have upon me as a treater. It has been a difficult chapter for me to write. I have felt an odd magnetic force, both attractive and repulsive. I have wondered about these polarities. For a while I thought that perhaps I was worried about what you, the reader, would think of me when you finish this segment. I believe that is too convenient an explanation. What really has pushed and pulled at my gut is wondering if I will like what I see as I brighten the lights on my own evil and good self. Like many people, I long to regard myself as a good person. I like to pretend that what evil might lurk within me is but a minute fraction of who I am. At most, I wish that my evil might be only a parenthetical comment or an insignificant footnote to a long chapter on my virtues. My task in this segment is to address cultural images of evil and good. In doing so I have had to wrestle with those same images within myself.

Before I get too immersed in writing about the images around us, I must remind you that I am a product of the post-World War II baby boom. A few years ago a patient described me as an over-the-hill flower child. With each passing year this epithet seems more and more accurate. I have been colored by the twists and turns our world has taken these past three or four decades. I know that my perceptions of what is good or bad are very different from those of my parents. I wonder if it was easier for them to distinguish right from wrong than it has been for me. In either case, I am convinced that it was different.

In the years just prior to my birth and the first ten years of my life, our American culture had a clear image of evil. Adolf Hitler and Nazi Germany had provided the world with a dramatic symbol of monstrous atrocity. Their horrific actions made it possible for everything malevolent to be projected upon them. The *Fuehrer* was the embodiment of all that was bad. In contrast, we Americans viewed ourselves as the symbol of virtue and goodness on the Earth. The American dream was a good one. In those years there was a reassuring sense that we had God on our side.

The benevolent self-image was challenged in the 1960s. Bob Dylan reflected upon this in song as he traced the nation's war history from the Spanish-American War through the Indian wars and the First World War—to end all wars—to the Second World War. A question is posed in the song: how did the Germans move from being such a dreaded enemy to close friend and ally in such a short period of time?

> *They murdered six million*
> *In the oven they fried*
> *The Germans now too*
> *Have God on their side*

The song goes on to recount the exchange of one enemy, Hitler's Germany, for another, Kruschev's Russia:

> *I've learned to hate Russia*
> *All through my whole life*
> *If another war starts*
> *It's them we must fight.*[17]

I can clearly remember the fear and hatred I had for the Russians as I was growing up. I recall going home from school one day in tears. Our teacher had explained in graphic detail the devastation caused by nuclear bombs and how Mr. Kruschev had pounded his shoe on the table at the United Nations and proclaimed, "We will bury you!" I was not yet ready to be buried. I also remember thinking that no matter how bad a boy I might be sometimes, at least my mommy must be glad that I'm no Russian. As you see, by the time I was in the third or fourth grade I had already learned that fine psychological defense of projection.

We baby boomers made it safely into high school, secure in the knowledge that Americans were good and Russians were bad; Zenith televisions were the best and things made in Japan were cheap imitations of American quality products. At about this same time the civil rights movement in America progressed from being an occasional irritating blister on our collective conscience to an ugly open wound. Scenes in the newspapers were vivid: George Wallace standing on the steps of a school, barring the entry of black children, freedom riders and burning buses, KKK rallies and crosses, and patrolmen clubbing unarmed men and women. Thanks to the media, these images would not go away.

There was growing dissension regarding American involvement in Viet Nam and the smug, self-righteous corporate view began to crack at its foundation. The images came into our living rooms every evening at six o'clock. Whether from the streets of Mobile or the dirt roads of the Qwang Nai district of Viet Nam, the disturbing subliminal message was, *All is not well in the American dreamland.*

Our culture experienced an unprecedented polarization. This is not to say that in our two hundred years there had never been division; but the presence of a television set in nearly every home in the nation made more people aware of, interested in or concerned about what was happening than ever before. This gave rise to slogans:

America, love it or leave it
Black Power
Better dead than red
Power to the people
Black is beautiful
If it feels good, do it
Hell no, we won't go
Peace now
Make love, not war
I have a dream

And one of my personal favorites of the time:

Never trust anyone over thirty

Some saw Martin Luther King as a saint
Some saw him as dangerous revolutionary
Some saw burning draft cards as courage
Some saw treason

Some saw the wisdom of Ghandi
Some saw the foolishness
Some saw the humor of the Smothers Brothers
Some saw need for censorship
Some saw George McGovern as a symbol of hope
Some saw a symbol of weakness
Some saw the Beatles more popular than Christ
Some saw the devil at work
Everyone saw the gaps, generational, racial, political, moral, religious.
 Everyone saw the gaps.

For us gap-ridden baby boomers things happened that forever altered our view of nation, culture and self. As we graduated from high school and moved on to college or the workplace, assassination attempts proliferated. Bobby Kennedy died. Martin Luther King died. George Wallace was paralyzed in an attempt on his life. On March 16, 1968, the Charlie Company moved into the hamlet of My Lai, rounded up and slaughtered between five and six hundred children, women and old men, none of whom were Viet Cong. On May 4, 1970, four college students were murdered by unknown members of the Ohio National Guard. In 1972 the nation was stunned by the precise disclosures of John Dean as he recounted the events of the burglary of the Watergate Hotel and the subsequent cover-up. Americans were bemused by the phrase "expletive deleted" in the transcripts of conversations of President Richard M. Nixon.

The common thread is that these events shook our trust in the goodness of those in authority and heightened our fear of the potential lunatic next door. It was no longer possible for our culture to point a finger at someone else's and proclaim it to be evil. We could take no comfort as we looked in the mirror for the old assurance of our goodness. For those who were open enough and willing to tolerate the pain of self-criticism and introspection, these events represented the death of innocence, giving birth to the Pogo cartoon message: "We have met the enemy and he is us."

Much of an entire generation lost faith in the powers that be, became convinced that our parents were wrong, were horrified by the maneuvers of the military-industrial complex and were disgusted by the bigots, hawks and tycoons of the United States. This disillusioned generation vowed with idealistic fervor to change the world. We marched here and there, volunteered, moved west, joined religious cults, communes, the Peace Corps and Vista. We developed a grandiose belief that our generation would not make the same mistakes as our parents. As a group, we mastered the psychological art of projection, even as I had done as a child.

The years rolled by. Race riots subsided. We gradually withdrew from Viet Nam. Nixon resigned. Somehow it seemed there was not much of anything around to protest anymore. One morning we woke and found ourselves with marriages, children, divorces, mortgages, two cars to a family and television with remote-controlled VCR. We play golf on Sunday mornings and tell off-color jokes. It is awfully hard to be sure who the good guys are anymore.

That all things we create are self-portraits is true not only for the individual artist but for the larger community as well. Perhaps the clearest mirror of present-day images of good and evil is the television screen. I flipped on my set (by remote control, of course) to collect some random impressions of the portrait. Here is some of what I saw:

Convenience is good. Convenient microwave dinners, convenient health maintenance providers, convenient early pregnancy tests, convenient douches, and, of course, convenience stores.

These things are bad: breath and body odors, headaches, telephone systems, menstrual cramps. A sports figure assured me that he never lets anyone see him sweat.

A soda pop commercial heralded the addition of caffeine to the product. I thought of a similar product's slogan about caffeine: *Never had it, never will!*

Two characters on a soap opera informed me that adultery is moral as long as your spouse doesn't find out.

A talk show host interviewed a millionaire televangelist who had recently been removed from his pulpit for sexual misconduct.

I really got lost. It is very hard to tell the Christians from the lions these days. I turned the television set off.

Convenience is good, inconvenience is bad. We seem to have lost our appreciation for struggle. Pain, discomfort and anxiety are conditions we take medications for rather than learn or grow from. One of the hallmarks of our era is that we do not value pain or adversity. We are deluged with pain-relief commercials that portray the desperation of a person before taking two little tablets, juxtaposed with a smiling, functional person only a few minutes after having done so. We like things to be easy—easy relationships, easy jobs, easy sex, easy fast-food, easy abortion, easy divorce, easy entertainment. We like to take life easy and we hope for an easy death. The great unspoken wish of our time is that our epitaph would read, *It was easy.*

Scott Peck begins his book, *The Road Less Traveled*, with the clear, straightforward sentence, "Life is difficult." When I read that sentence for the first time, a wave of relief washed over me. It was the kind of relief that comes with the awareness that someone else understands how you feel. At last I knew that I was not alone in my belief that life was hard. Having grown up in the dream years of the fifties and come of age in the turbulent idealism of the sixties and seventies, I had a vague sense of dis-ease for a long time. I had been sold the notion that life would be better for me than it had been for my parents who had survived the Great Depression. Myriad overt and covert communications gave me a feeling of effortless entitlement to good things. The older I got, the more I began to feel that something was wrong with me. Life was not all that easy. In fact, by the time I was in my mid-twenties I was fairly convinced that it was hard. Doctor Peck's three words were a deep reassurance that it was okay not to have things too easy.

It takes a lot of energy to wrestle with images of evil and good, whether in the larger world or within the self. Simply thinking about the possibilities can be overwhelming. In a prophetic social commentary, *The Sane Society*, Erich Fromm writes:

> Man today is confronted with the most fundamental choice . . . between robotism (of both the capitalist and communist variety), or Humanistic Communitarian Socialism. Most facts seem to indicate that he is choosing robotisms, and that means, in the long run, insanity and destruction. But all these facts are not strong enough to destroy faith in man's reason, good will and sanity. As long as we can think of alternatives we are not lost; as long as we can consult together and plan together, we can hope. But, indeed, the shadows are lengthening; the voices . . . are becoming louder.[26]

The fundamental choice that Doctor Fromm defines is made not only on the societal/political level but must be made by individuals as well. In that, I see the continuing lengthening of shadows and I hear the rising voices.

Still, I am not pessimistic about our culture. Though there is much evidence of our hedonism and shallow materialism, I am yet hopeful because of the artists of the world. The artist—acclaimed professional, dabbling amateur or struggling patient—still seems to be interested in skirmishing with evil and good. It was, after all, the musicians and poets (Dylan, Baez, The Beatles) that shook the conscience of America and generated the emotional energy required to resist and protest the Viet Nam war. It was the writers, Woodward and Bernstein, who had the courage to face the powerful in Washington and tell the story of Watergate. It was Picasso who painted "Guernica"; Dali who painted "Soft Construction with Boiled Beans: Premonition of Civil War." In each case it was an artist who gave the world a lyrical, verbal or visual image to stir our conscience.

More recently the musician Sting wrote:

> *We share the same biology*
> *regardless of ideology.*
> *Believe me when I say to you*
> *I hope the Russians love their children too.*[27]

We can all truly hope that somewhere in Moscow a counterpart sings to his audience, *I hope the Americans love their children too.*

At every twist and turn of history it has been the painter, the poet, the playwright who has been willing to struggle with what he saw around him in the world. The artist has always been the one willing to be wounded as he wrestles with the forces of evil and good. Willing to tolerate the pain of public criticism, censorship and rejection, the artist has perceived and spoken, nevertheless. There has been something intrinsic to the artist that has kept him from bowing to pressure from whatever source.

The intrinsic element is the nature of the artistic process. I return to H. W. Janson's metaphor of birth to describe the making of art. It begins in an act of love, sometimes tender, sometimes aggressive, sometimes pleasurable, sometimes frightening. Birthing is painful, joyous and full of surprises, but mostly it is damn hard work and struggle. When I was in seminary, one of my professors said, "If you don't absolutely have to be a minister, for God's sake don't be one." The same is true of artists; if they did not have to be, they would not.

Creating art has a way of comforting when the artist is in pain and afflicting when the artist could be comfortable. I see this time and again in my clinical work and this is where my real hope for our culture is born. I see patients in great emotional pain draw out their evil monsters and tame them. I watch as their heroic selves move from within to hand to chalk to paper. I listen as they tell their stories and I hear them abandon their meaningless blaming of others, welcoming a courageous acceptance of responsibility for their own lives. At my best I participate in helping tell their projections of good and bad in others and act as a midwife in their birth struggle. Sometimes I become a temporary foe with whom they do creative, healing battle. At other times I am only an attentive audience invested in understanding the meaning of the dreams unfolding before me.

Just as their historic artistic predecessors such as Francisco Goya, Henri Rousseau, Edvard Munch and others were willing and able to face the monsters of their time, so too my patients engage theirs. Sometimes the demons are too powerful and the play ends tragically. Sometimes the victory is glorious or the truce admirable. Regardless of the outcome I am repeatedly awed by the struggle my patient/artists are able to muster. My hope is that our culture will do the same; that we will cease the defensive process of looking for enemies to embody evil in order to delude ourselves about our own goodness.

There is hope for all of us. If you really want to understand balancing on the cutting edge of evil and good, I suggest you take out your paints, your pen, whatever, and start by looking in the mirror. Then let yourself struggle to create. I suspect that you will find all the things that are evil in the world lurking somewhere inside you, and I predict that for every dragon you find, there will be a St. George close behind. More than anything else I would hope that you experience the wisdom of Thomas Aquinas, who said, "Virtue stands in the middle."

The crucial point of this for us therapists is that we can deal with the evil, the monstrous or ugly ruined parts of our patients only by knowing and accepting those same parts of ourselves. In a paper dealing with this topic, Cathy Moon used the metaphor of the compost pile:

> I stand back for a moment to look at what I have just done. The bright orange carrot, red apple peels, the shards of white eggshells almost dazzle as they sit atop that pile. And yet they stink . . . Now sitting atop this mound of weeds, horse manure and decomposing food they have new possibility. What is rotting and stinking will become nourishing, give new life. . . . If I am to stay honest in this art therapy business then I must also be constantly in touch with my own garbage, my own evil. The image I have is of myself reaching inward, gingerly, reluctantly pulling out slime, venom, oozing mud. It stinks. I do not like it but I cannot shake it off my hands. There is nothing left to do but hold it, be with it, try to love it.

An Introspection

I have already told you that I have been invested in maintaining the notion that I am a good person. I want you to think that I am, and further I want to think that I am. For many of my thirty-six years it has been relatively easy to maintain this view. I grew up a good Methodist boy who went to church and sang in the choir, got good grades and played football. I never got anyone pregnant that I was not supposed to. I made what I considered to be the right moral choices by being a conscientious objector during the Viet Nam war. I even went so far as to spend several years of my life in a seminary and I chose to go into a helping profession.

As happens in most lives, however, things came up along the way that I never expected, did not plan for and really did not want. Such things inevitably arose in Cathy's and my life together. During that time I kept a journal of how I was feeling. The pages of that book were for me a safety valve as I wrestled with internal forces and feelings that I had never before acknowledged. I painted a lot, too, but the paintings were an affliction, no comfort at all. It was a terrible time for me as I struggled with my anger directed at Cathy and at the same time found myself sickened by the intense rage and vulnerability within myself. Not only were there relationship issues with her to deal with, but a relationship with an ugly hateful monster in me whom I had never met.

As I sat in my truck one day writing about all this, suddenly the image came to me of *a gift.* I almost laughed out loud at this ludicrous image. How in hell can this period of my life be a gift? But the image would not go away. As I wrote on, it occurred to me that the gift was given to me by Cathy. That evening when I got home, when the kids were asleep and we had time, I read her the poem. We both cried and held each other. As I look back I believe that I . . . we began to heal our relationship.

In the years that have passed I have continued to struggle with the gift, with what it meant and what it means. Some thoughts are that Cathy and I have grown up a lot; we have learned to accept and love the whole of ourselves and each other most of the time. I've come to know myself as a person, not a lone chapter of virtue with parenthetical commentary. I've learned to accept that life does not always play out of my Pollyanna script. We've become acquainted with the depths of our own evil, which has had a tremendous impact on our capacity for good.

An Artist on the Edge: A Man and His Demon

When I first met Denny he was a man in mental and emotional agony. He came to the hospital after having isolated himself for several months. He had a long history of bizarre behavior, including episodes of explosive aggression towards others, self-mutilation by burning, and taking walks in the woods unclothed and many other extraordinary actions. This was his first hospitalization and at first it was thought that he was severely depressed, perhaps in a psychotic depression. His early hospital treatment was complicated by the fact that he had allergic reactions to the major tranquilizers Haldol and Thorazine.

As he grew more comfortable and trusting of his psychiatrist and the nursing staff, the severity of his illness emerged. He clearly experienced periods of dissociation and depersonalization. He exhibited delusional thoughts of both a persecutory and grandiose nature.

Denny's doctor and the nursing staff were very concerned about his inability to function in the daily life of the cottage as well as in therapeutic activities off the unit. He spent the majority of his time alone in his room or secluded in special care when his thoughts and behavior demanded a destimulating, safe and containing environment. The inability to use helpful medications made it very difficult to provide Denny with any contact with people.

During a team discussion about these concerns, I suggested that we might try involving Denny in my expressive art group. This ran counter to the team's philosophy which was that creative expression of feeling was not appropriate for individuals with thought disorders. The team was concerned that expressive art might further weaken already shakey ego boundaries and put Denny at further risk of being overwhelmed by feelings and impulses. In short, art would only make the patient more crazy. Although I understood the team's theoretical perspective, I argued that art can often be a structuring element and that in fact creating art is an organizing process, not the converse. This caused a fair amount of controversy on the team, and I was relatively new on the staff. Eventually, the psychiatrist intervened and said that he would keep my recommendation in mind, but for the present he did not want to rock the boat.

Over the next few weeks, Denny's isolation increased and he seemed to withdraw even further into his own world. Again, the team expressed concern for how little contact he had with anyone other than the staff. One nurse shared that she had noticed some "weird drawings" crumpled up in his wastebasket. The psychiatrist turned to me and revived the idea of using art as a way to communicate with Denny. He suggested, however, that entering Denny into a group would probably not be advisable. He asked if I would be able to meet with Denny one to one. I quickly agreed, little realizing that it would begin a relationship that would span over two years of our lives.

In our first session I set the parameters for our meetings by explaining that I would come to the unit twice each week for a half hour and that I would bring drawing materials with me. I also told him that if he drew things at other times, I would be most interested in seeing his work, if he wanted to share it. Although he did not speak to me, his body movements were strangely contradictory. His face brightened as I laid the newsprint and chalks on the table, yet he appeared to shrink from me.

Using these nonverbal messages as significant indicators as to how to proceed, I gave Denny a sheet of paper and asked him to draw on the theme of "tug of war." The drawing that emerged was overwhelming in its raw statement of turmoil. The drawing presented two representations of Denny: one in white and one in black, both clutching desperately a fraying rope. At the opposite end of the rope were eight demons, pulling madly. Between the two teams was a black, smoking pit.

As Denny completed the drawing he was sweating profusely and shaking. I asked him if he felt ill. "No," he said, "it's just the screaming all the time. I don't know if I can stand it."

"Who is screaming, Denny?"

He pointed to the demons. "Them. Always them."

We discussed the drawing and several interesting aspects were revealed. Each of the demons had a name and a well-developed role to play in Denny's world. They had been with him for a long time, but before doing this drawing he had never told anyone about them. He assured me that Denny-white was a good person, studious, intelligent and gentle. Denny-black was strong, aggressive and protective. All of the characters in this drama were well acquainted with each of the others. The first drawing set the stage for what was to be a colossal war that would be waged within Denny for the next several years.

Near the end of our first hour together Denny huddled in a corner of the room and clapped his hands over his ears. "Tell them to shut up," he shouted. He thrust his foot toward the drawing. "They're so loud."

"Denny," I said, "you can make them be quiet. This is your drawing. You drew it, you created it."

"Ah! I can't."

"You created it, Denny. If you want them to be quiet, tear the drawing off the wall."

"I can't," he screamed.

"Denny, you are the master of what you draw."

His sweating intensified, he rocked and shook in the corner. "I can't touch it," he sobbed. "If I touch it they will never let me go."

I could see how deeply he was being affected, so I slowly went to the wall where his drawing was.

"Don't!" he shouted. "They'll burn you."

"I am not afraid of them, Denny. I see them for who they are." With that, I gently removed the anchoring tape and rolled the drawing into a tight tube and taped it shut.

Immediately his quivering ceased. His breathing gradually returned to normal and he relaxed his pose. He looked at me awestruck as I sat with the paper roll in my hand. "I can barely hear them. Their voices are all muffled. You took them away. . . . "

"Maybe for a little while, Denny. I believe that you created them and then somehow they took over. We have to get them back in perspective."

"Do you think I'm crazy?"

"Denny, I just saw what you feel inside. I don't know if it's crazy. I know it is painful and hard for you."

For the next year Denny continued to draw his demons and his white and black sides. He gradually moved from individual sessions to being able to be in an expressive group. We got to know his tormentors well. One demon was the holder of fire. This devil's task was to contain Denny's rage. Another demon was the holder of sexual feelings. Still another bore all the hurt Denny had experienced growing up in a strict religious and yet physically and emotionally abusive family. Another demon consistently blamed Denny for all his misfortunes.

Denny's psychiatrist theorized that in the course of Denny's life each of the demons had been symbolically created in an effort to compartmentalize feelings and thoughts that he was not able or allowed to express to his family. The doctor viewed the devils as a metaphoric coping mechanism, i.e., a desperate attempt to maintain some semblance of balance in a terribly destructive environment. Thus the frame for understanding Denny was built on viewing his adaptive style as healthy rather than labeling it sick or crazy.

Through the progression of months, the demons became less horrific and threatening images. They eventually lost their demonic form altogether, transformed into symbolic images of the powerful feelings which had given them birth. At the completion of every drawing, Denny ritually insisted that I roll them up and keep them in my office.

Gradually, the devilish images were exchanged for more direct expressions of feelings, and the distance between Denny-white and Denny-black came more sharply into focus. Where Denny-white engaged in the study of philosophy, theology and chess, Denny-black dominated the game on the volleyball court, cracked raunchy jokes and lifted weights.

The treatment team had all but resigned itself to the possibility that this separation, compartmentalization or split, might be so indigenous that it would not mend. It did not take into account the powerful role that fate can play in the lives of people.

It happened that during a week when Denny's case manager was away at a conference, a close friend of his was tragically killed. The treatment team met early that morning to wrestle with who should tell Denny about the death. We were all very concerned because news of the tragedy had been broadcast on the radio and we felt sure it would be on the evening television news and surely in the next day's newspaper. No one wanted Denny to learn of it this way. After much discussion it was decided that I should be the one to share the news with him, and I did.

We sat in the studio for several minutes in silence. I had expected an outburst of some kind, crying or yelling, or disbelief. But there was silence. Then Denny-white began a long monologue on how difficult his friend's life had been; how maybe there was peace for him now and perhaps it was all for the best. He rambled on and on, quite intellectual, quite unaffected. After several minutes I stopped him in mid-sentence. I told him that I was concerned about his calm and rational manner. He agreed that it was troubling to him, too, but he could not find any feelings inside. I suggested that we draw.

The image is one that I will never forget. On one side of the paper was a representation of his friend and an ocean with an empty life jacket bobbing in the water. Hovering above the turbulent sea was an image of Denny-white being struck by lightning.

He sat down, trembling. I asked him to give the drawing a sound. He screamed, a long, haunting howl. When he ran out of breath, tears filled his eyes. "I can't take this, I can't take this!" he cried.

"But you have no choice," I said.

"Why does everything good have to die?"

"I don't know, Denny."

Denny stood up and with a purple chalk moved to his paper again. He drew another person standing behind the image of Denny-white. The purple figure's hands were placed on the shoulders of Denny-white.

"What's happening?" I asked.

"I'll strangle that weakling."

"It looks more like the purple guy is rubbing the other's shoulders," I observed.

"What?" said Denny.

"The dark one, Denny . . . looks like he's comforting you, consoling you."

Denny pulled back his fist from the paper and slammed it against the image of the empty life jacket. He wept and wept.

Denny's journey was a long and arduous one. We walked together for a little more than two years. The focus of his pilgrimage was constant: to integrate the opposing forces within himself. His demons were exorcised through the expressive process, both in his psychiatrist's office and in the art studio. We learned to know them by name, and once they were clearly identified, they lost their malevolent hold on him. Denny-white and Denny-black were in the end able to embrace each other. Denny-white was strengthened by the power and aggressiveness of Denny-black. Denny-black was tamed by the sensitive intellect of Denny-white.

As the time neared for us to end our relationship we talked about how to bring it to a close. After a variety of options had been aired and discarded, Denny asked if I still had all of his drawings. I assured him that I did. He suggested that we might get together and take a look back at all the things he had created. I had never counted the drawings, but there must have been a hundred or more. We sat in a meeting room and one by one unrolled and scanned history. Denny grew agitated. With each drawing his discomfort grew.

"Denny, do we need to stop?" I asked.

"No, it's just all the memories, all the pain."

"It's been a tough road."

"Yeah, yeah it has."

At last, with all the drawings unrolled, helter-skelter on the floor, we sat in silence and beheld the artifacts of our journey into hell and back. "This isn't right," Denny said, "I should feel better . . . I mean, I always thought that when my therapy was over I'd feel good."

"Saying goodbye to you is hard, Denny," I said.

"This is like some kind of a board meeting or something. All these old nightmares and pieces of me all sitting here. It feels weird."

"Maybe the board members aren't in their proper places yet," I offered. "What do you mean?" he asked.

"Well, I think that executive boards of corporations probably have some kind of assigned seating order, like the president at the head of the table, the vice-president on the right, the treasurer on the left, or something like that. How should your board be arranged?"

Denny spent several minutes rearranging his drawings. Some he rolled up, some he taped to chairs and a few he laid face down under the table. Finally he turned to me. "Bruce, you sit here," and he pointed to a chair near the head of the table. "You are the creative consultant to the firm." He sighed as he stepped back to survey the dramatic still life he had created. "I wish I had a camera."

I got some film from the departmental supply and loaded a camera. Denny took the picture—a board meeting of all the terrors and heroes of two years of his life.

Chapter XI

THE CHANGING FACE OF ILLNESS

The emotional and mental difficulties that confront us today are quite different from those that challenged Sigmund Freud and Carl Jung because of the complex interrelation of individual dynamics and their societal/cultural context. Through Freud's careful study of his patients in the Victorian era much information was gathered about the makeup of psyche and personality. From the perspective of specific pathologies was born Freud's view of individual dynamics. Today, we seldom see the classic pictures of symptomatology such as phobia or hysteria described by Freud and others. We are far more likely to encounter existential emptiness or boredom, the vague sense that nothing is worthwhile and everything is meaningless. The genuinely exciting frontrunners of psychotherapeutic thinking are focused now on the developmental formation of borderline and narcissistic disorders, of which the hallmark is the lack of authentic relatedness to others.

These relatively new diseases have moved the emphasis from *id*-oriented psychologies to *ego* psychology. Object relations theorists have focused our attention on the subtleties of the emotional climate between infant and mother, toddler and nurturer. The spotlight falls upon these early developmental experiences precisely at a period when mothering as a role has been somewhat devalued when juxtaposed with the emerging role of women in the workplace. Simultaneously, the ability of a family to survive comfortably on the income of one wage earner is increasingly rare. There has been a disruption in societal support for the mother role.

The origins of emotional dysfunction are multifaceted. Components of genetics, biology, family milieu, natural and cultural factors along with fate and intra- and interpersonal colorations are the ingredients of those who would theorize about the psyche.

From the viewpoint of an existential art therapist, I would like to explore this turbulent mix of etiological factors as they apply to what I consider to be the dominant pathology of our era, borderline personality. I will also focus on a specific symptom of this illness, ahistoricity, which I

117

believe is directly related to the changing face of psychiatric distur-
bances brought on by powerful changes in our culture.

Discussions within the modern psychiatric hospital or clinic revolve
around diagnosis, measurable goals and justification to third-party payors
much more than around symbol, existence or personhood. I have deep
misgivings about this pragmatic focus, so I am hesitant to write about a
specific diagnostic category, i.e., #301.83 in your DSM–III–R manual.
When I first began my career as an art therapist I enjoyed labeling.
Naively, I thought that if I could put the right name on something I
could make it better. It would all make sense. I loved words like
schizophrenia, melancholia and neurosis. I felt wise when I could say to
myself after meeting a new patient, "Ah, this is a manic-depressive in a
manic phase." It gave me a wonderful feeling of omniscience when I later
read the patient's chart and confirmed my diagnostic accuracy. Labels
gave me a sense of control and security. In our Judeo-Christian tradition
there is a story in which God is said to have created a universe full of
creatures and things by naming them. In my novice days I experienced a
bit of godliness as I labeled those with whom I came in contact.

Fifteen years later I am less enamored of names, less able to be
comforted by precise labels. In fact, I have grown uneasy with my clinical
jargon. I no longer feel freed by clinical description. On the contrary, I
often encounter a sense of entrapment by category.

> *Don't talk of love*
> *I've heard the word before*
> *It's sleeping in my memory*
> *I won't disturb the slumber*
> *Of feelings that have died*
> *If I'd never loved*
> *I never would have cried*
> *I am a rock*
> *I am an island*

Paul Simon[28]

Perhaps an acceptable third line to the chorus of this well-known
poem could be *I am a borderline.*

I am intrigued by these rocky island, fortress folks. They always seem
to get the hook into *me* as I go about casting my therapeutic nets in hopes
of pulling *them* into treatment. Their hooks are razor-sharp and barbed.
They often tear my emotional flesh. I have spent a lot of time looking in

the mirror, wondering why I so readily volunteer for such potentially painful expeditions.

I have some notions about why borderlines inspire such feelings in me, why they are so adept at engaging me and others in their turmoil. They seem to remind me how precious my time is and they expose my vulnerabilities in ways I cannot escape.

A few years ago I attended a lecture by Doctor James Masterson in which he outlined the concept of abandonment depression in borderline pathology. In essence, the patient is forced to act out the abandonment trauma of the past constantly in the present. This is because of the borderline's inability to conceive relationships as a whole but, rather, as an unconnected string of parts. The disconnection from past relationships causes them to deal with each relationship strictly in the present.

In relating to others, the patient has no past, only the here and now. It is safe to presume that in addition to the absence of a past, the borderline patient likewise has no belief or faith in the future. Their actions in the present carry power not unlike that of the primitive man. Their rocky island of personhood, perhaps the whole of existence, rests on what they do right now. How dramatic!

The dramatic intensity of the visible outline of the symptoms of ahistoricity is seen profoundly in borderlines. In today's world, traditional sources of groundedness and our sense of continuity, even identity itself, are faltering or extinct. In times past, the church, the family, the hometown all coalesced to provide a sense of one's place in the stream of life. There was a sense that one's individual and communal future was predictable and could be relied upon. The old boundaries have been shattered as the pace of societal change has become dizzying. The nuclear family is in jeopardy. The extended family has been fractured by the mobility of the individual. During a presentation on this subject I asked for a show of hands of persons in the audience who lived in the town they had grown up in. I followed this by asking how many lived within one hundred miles of their grandparents. Only a fraction of the people raised their hands for either question. Few of us are rooted in these ways. All the many changes, coupled with the omnipresent awareness that humankind has created the means for its own catastrophic destruction, has left us with a cultural gestalt of disembodiment from the past and skepticism about the future. We have become an era of ahistoricity. Each generation must form its own identity, a dislocated blip on the time line, without reference or relationship to points before it or after it...a generation stuck in the present.

When we of western civilization think about time or try to visualize and describe time, we generally imagine the time line concept that we have been taught in school, church everywhere . . . that somehow history had a beginning and will have an end. The time line, however, is a relatively new idea in the history of humankind. There is considerable evidence that prior to the writing of the Torah, time was viewed quite differently. Primitive man would have been more likely to think of time as a circle. Phases of the moon, menstrual cycles, the four seasons and the life cycle itself would have illustrated a non-linear perspective. Consequently, primitive people would not have understood us as we talk about looking back to last year or looking forward to tomorrow, since for them all time was present. Just as there is no beginning point on a circle because all points are connected, so, too, all time is present in each moment.

In the novel *Dead Eye Dick* by Kurt Vonnegut,[29] there is a minor character, an islander. His primitive language has only the present tense. The main character, Dick, is both amused and vaguely uneasy as the islander asks about a woman who has died, "How is she?"

To be always in the present tense is the plight of the borderline. In relating to others they have no sense of what will be. They experience the departure of their therapist for a week's vacation as earth shattering, like the struggle of the toddler to survive outside the sphere of the mother.

While we rational, healthy, *normal* people must always contend with our past and future, in effect diluting our experience of the present, the borderline patient embodies dramatic, intense immediacy. This can cause the treater to have a vague sense of envy, a flickering mirror image of our lives as they were way back when. It was my friend and colleague John Reece who first sensitized me to the scope of this drama as he and I wrote a paper together, *Victims, Villain and Heroes: Treatment Metaphors of Borderline Patients*, in 1980. In that work we formulated the view that the borderline is a living, breathing metaphor . . . *rocky islands of existence*.

The wisdom of thousands of years of humankind's struggle to understand itself, to be with others and find meaning in life has too often been replaced with the search for measurable goals and scientifically verifiable data. We have reduced beyond recognition the concerns that make us most human and we miss our life's metaphors.

During the writing of this book, Doctor Marcel Hundziak, a child psychiatrist, stopped me in the hospital corridor one day to ask how the work was going. He complimented me on my interest in existentialism. "This is good," he said in his eastern European accent, "we need always to remember the deeper things." The exchange encouraged me. It reinforced my love of metaphor.

The dangers of discussing metaphor reside in verbal denotations. Because I am an existential art therapist, I am attuned to the use of action metaphors. The art therapist's essential contribution to the treatment of borderline patients is our sensitivity to and ability to interact with our patients symbolically through metaphor, ritual and action. Before exploring the specific role of the arts and art therapy with these patients, I will briefly review the theoretical framework of the etiology of the borderline personality.

Current understanding of this disorder is rooted in *object relations theory*, which deals with the infant's development of reality perception and understanding as well as the ability to form relationships and accurately perceive other people in relationship to himself. In the first three months of life the infant's relationship with his mother is one of symbiosis. In his perception of reality there is no separation of himself and mother. There is no separation of self and object, i.e., mother. He is said at this time to lack ego boundaries, or the awareness of where he stops and his environment begins.

In the following months, he gradually attains a sense of separateness from his environment, a necessary task for accurate reality testing in the future. It is theorized that the failure of this task at this early stage results in schizophrenic disorders, in which the adult is unable to demonstrate stable ego boundaries.

During the first three months of the infant's life he has essentially two emotional states: one that corresponds to the feeling of being fed, held and nurtured; the other that is connected with the experience of being wet, cold, hungry or lonely. The first state is the source of all later pleasurable emotions and is libidinal, having connection with the pleasure-seeking drive. The second state is rage and it is the progenitor of all later negative feelings connected with the aggressive drive.

In addition to forming ego boundaries, the infant past the age of three months has the task of connecting negative and positive experiences in such a way as to give a real picture of himself and his world. Until this time he has been able through the primitive ego process of splitting to

primitive process of SPLITTING

keep his affective experiences of pleasure and rage entirely separate in his consciousness. When he is in the affective state of pleasure, it is as if the bad feeling state never exists. When he is in a state of rage, he has no experience of ever feeling any differently.

The twofold task of the infant ego at this stage is to achieve an awareness of his separateness from his environment and to achieve a unity of perception of himself and his environment, whether it is charged with bad or good affective tones. The first task is crucial to the development of object constancy, the ability to maintain a single image of an object (or himself), whether it is bad or good, present or absent. In the normal infant these tasks are accomplished and the infant ego is able to go on without undue conflict to accomplish further tasks of development.

It is at this stage of beginning object constancy that there is a defect in the development of the borderline. While the borderline is able to form adequate ego boundaries, he is generally unable to demonstrate genuine object constancy, with consequent disruption of the relationship between himself and his world. Let us examine the process of this developmental flaw.

During this crucial stage, separation-individuation, the infant begins to explore his environment away from his mother, which eventually leads to his ability to form ego boundaries. The mother, with whom the infant's emotions are still intimately connected, has a profound effect upon the affective tone of this stage. If we presume some disruption of the processes of separation-individuation, we can theorize the later disruptions of life in the individual.

The infant, at least at the beginning of this stage, still employs the early ego process, splitting, that serves to keep separate experiences in differing affective tone. It is theorized that if the infant's experience of rage at this stage is strong or frequent enough the splitting process becomes entrenched. It takes on the attributes of a defense mechanism rather than giving way normally to a more developed defense mechanism of repression. Masterson suggests that the development of splitting as a defensive maneuver can arise from nature, nurture or fate. In the first instance, we can hypothesize an infant with a genetically determined low frustration tolerance that could lead to an individual experience of frequent or severe rage. In the fate example, one can hypothesize a catastrophe such as death of the mother, war, natural disaster, interrupting this developmental stage and charging it with negative emotion. Believed to be most common is the circumstance where the infant's relationship with mother is constrained by the mother's own pathology. The mother is frequently borderline herself.

In this example, the mother is unable because of her own pathology to reinforce the ego tasks of the separation-individuation stage. Instead, she rewards the infant when he behaves in the earlier symbiotic fashion, and withdraws love when the infant makes attempts to individuate. The result is an inability on the infant's part to combine images of good and bad mother into a stable entity and therefore he is unable to achieve object constancy.

These two basic flaws in the infant's developing ego—(1) the retention of splitting as a defense mechanism and (2) the failure to achieve object constancy—provide the basis for the mass of related symptoms that later characterize the borderline patient.

The retention of splitting is a commonly seen manifestation of the borderline's illness. It is at the hub of a swirl of related, repetitive symptoms. The best-known feature of the splitting defense is the division of people in the borderline's world into all good and all bad. It is also responsible for the abrupt reversals of the borderline's feelings about a particular person from one extreme to the other, with no apparent memory or awareness on the patient's part of the feelings ever being any different.

Splitting is also related to what Kernberg calls "primitive idealization" in which the patient sees another as all good in order to protect himself against the "bad" persons. There is no real regard for the revered one but rather a simple need for it in a world of bad and dangerous people.

Projective identification is another frequently seen manifestation of borderline illness. Also related to splitting, it is the placement by the borderline patient of his own internal rage feelings into his environment, which is then seen to be dangerous, threatening and chaotic. Because of the intensity of the aggressive feelings invested here, the normally adequate ego boundaries are weakened, allowing this particular loss of reality testing and lack of differentiation between self and object. The common behavioral effect of this mechanism in the clinical setting is the patient's attempt to control the behavior of those he feels are threatening him.

The final aspect of splitting is the combination of omnipotence and devaluation. The borderline patient using these two mechanisms may shift between needing to establish a clinging relationship with another who, for the patient, has magical powers, and devaluing or dismissing that person when the patient's needs are not being met. The idealized person is actually used as a defensive object by the patient, as an extension of the patient's needs. There is a need to control the idealized person, to manipulate him or her into defending the borderline against projected aggression. If the external object (idealized person) can provide no further gratification or protection, it is dismissed and devalued because the patient'didn't really love it in the first place." Devaluation is also important to the patient to prevent the rejected ones from becoming feared and hated persecutors.

Lack of object constancy comes into play as a specific defect when, for example, a therapist goes on vacation. The patient is unable to produce an image of the departed one in memory and therefore feels as though the person is forever gone. This is frequently internalized emotionally by the patient as willful abandonment, with the rage and sorrow accompanying this situation that is observable in the patient's behavior.

A true lack of object constancy means also that borderline patients will be unable to mourn for significant persons who have indeed died and abandoned them. They cannot feel anything like normal grief and are unable to deal with the feelings that accompany such a loss. Moreover, since a borderline's memory does not carry past images of positive relationships, they are unable to trust that such relationships are possible in the present or future. They are forced to deal in fantastic ways with only a present-tense, moment-by-moment world of relationship with others. Their world is a single-present moment filled with threat, anxiety, emptiness, unreality and magic, and they are stuck in it.

So what are we therapists to do for these stuck, empty and angry people? There was a period of time when the mental health authorities believed that there was little that could be done. Perhaps they believed we could only be there to sew up the self-inflicted physical and emotional wounds, then send them on their way until the next crisis. This is not my view, for I have been a part of the successful treatment of borderlines. I have witnessed their creation of a personal history. And I have ached with them as they tentatively spread their roots. All of this has happened as part of our relationship in which I have engaged in tasks with them, been open to them and honored their pain as the journey proceeded.

A Story of Wealth

Kerry was hospitalized after having recovered from the physical injuries she had sustained in an automobile accident. She had driven her car into a concrete bridge support. She had been drinking on the night of the accident and there were conflicting reports of what had happened. Kerry and her parents had an argument that day and they claimed she had threatened suicide. Kerry vehemently denied any intent to harm herself.

Her family was quite wealthy and, although Kerry was twenty-one years old and a full-time college student, she still lived at home. By all accounts she was an overindulged and spoiled girl who had always gotten whatever she wanted, whenever she wanted it.

The primary focus of her treatment team was Kerry's resistance to emancipation. She would have panic attacks whenever the notion of moving away from her loving, engulfing parents was mentioned. Treaters from each discipline had confronted her self-defeating and self-destructive dependence on her parents, to no avail.

She entered my expressive arts psychotherapy group after several weeks of treatment in our hospital. Her position was still firm: (a) nothing was wrong, she had no reason to be there; (b) the auto accident had been just that, nothing more; and (c) discussion of her relationship with her parents would not be tolerated.

In the early sessions of her participation in the expressive group, I found myself angry at her stubborn denial that her relationship with her parents had anything to do with the variety of destructive behaviors she had manifested. As I listened to her describe her drawings and dialogued with them, I was reminded of my own feelings of insecurity and abandonment during my own emancipation. Though the circumstances of our lives were quite different, the feelings were not. How dare she make me remember those difficult years!

I began the next session of the group with a story:

Outside a certain town at a certain time not too long ago, a man ran out of gas for his car. As he walked toward town with his gas can in hand, he came upon a horrible sight. Beside a rundown old house there was a rundown old dog house. An old dog lay in front of it, licking a wound in its side. The man was moved with pity and approached the dog. The closer he got the more evidence of maltreatment he could see. The animal was filthy and scarred. One eye was swollen shut. The man was appalled. He said to the dog, "Oh, you poor thing." Since this was a magical place the dog raised his head and replied, "Are you talking to me?" The man said, "Yes. My God, how did you get to be such a mess?" Without hesitation the dog responded, "It's my master. He has many stresses in his life and when he comes home at the end of the day he often beats me to relieve his tension." The man felt anger mix with his pity. "Well, why do you stay here? Your collar is rotted; surely you could break it and run away." The dog blinked his one good eye and said, "But he always feeds me so well."

I asked the group to draw out their responses to the story. Kerry's drawing was filled with rage at the dog's master. At one point in the discussion that followed, she blurted out, "Well, all I have to say is that food must be darn good!"

Another patient in the group turned toward Kerry and calmly asked, "Well, Kerry, how good is it?" Kerry fumed momentarily, then laughed, then cried. She had discovered a truth about her life in the metaphor of a mistreated dog. To be sure, her parents had never beaten her, but they had stunted her emotional growth by overprotecting and overindulging her. They had at every turn rewarded her for not growing up. They had fostered her inappropriate dependence upon them. Their food was so good. Her insight marked the end of her overt resistance to exploring issues of emancipation.

This session also altered her perception of me. I had been categorized as a vicious, cold and insensitive person in her world. Suddenly, I became a knight in shining armor, an ally. Her treatment in the group then focused on reconciling these two greatly differing views of me. On her last day in the group she drew a gift for me. Describing it, she said, "You are just a man. I like you. I don't hate you and I don't love you." It was a fine gift.

Chapter XII

WHAT IS THE PAST?

Donna was admitted to the hospital when she was sixteen years old. The presenting problems for her were: oppositional behavior, stealing, defiance of authority and lying. She is the offspring of a teenage mother of the 1970s. Donna's parents had lived with Donna's grandmother for several years after her birth. Generational boundaries and familial roles were blurred for much of that time. When Donna's mother became pregnant with Donna's brother, the family at last moved out on its own. Soon after the birth of the brother Donna's parents separated and eventually divorced. Both parents soon remarried, and custody of Donna has been in flux throughout the years. Donna told us that she had moved at least seven or eight times that she could remember. She said her problems were because of her lack of friends.

Donna's ahistoricity was dramatically evident as attempts were made to gather information about her past. Even with the visual stimulation of childhood photographs supplied by her mother she could not muster any affective memory. For Donna and many other ahistorical adolescents, the focus of treatment is the question: how do we help the ahistorical patient create an identity with a past? How can the hospital serve the patient in the same way that a rooting jar serves a plant cutting ... by becoming a safe, nurturing place to grow roots? These questions have implications for each part of the clinical team.

As the art therapist on the treatment team, I began to pay closer attention to the apparent natural attraction these patients have to the doing of art. They are the spontaneous artists on the unit. Often, at their own initiation, they keep a personal sketchbook which becomes a nonverbal diary. The striking thing is that while these patients are often quite resistive in many areas of treatment, they require no luring at all to draw. It is as if their images push their way out. There is something dramatically immediate in creating art that reverberates within the emptiness of the ahistorical patient. The intense pleasure and pain and struggle stimulated by the creative birthing process is the here-and-now hook that

127

catches the patient's imagination and investment. It is an encounter with the world which both echoes and transcends their dramatic *nowness.* Every image the artist creates is a fragment of a continuously evolving self-portrait. For the artist/patient this is significant as he gradually discovers and owns his metaphoric representations of self.

Keeping in mind H. W. Janson's[19] notion of a web of art built on the traditions of all that has gone before it, we observe that Donna and others like her begin to claim aspects of self through art. Simultaneously, a relationship is symbolically established with history. The real task in the art studio is to help the patient develop a sense of curiosity about his own roots and to engage him in the joy of self-discovery. The beauty of art in relating to this task is its action/metaphoric, ritual nature. The ritual provides the safety needed for so difficult a journey.

In essence I attempt to engage the ahistorical, borderline adolescent in a metaphorical self-birthing event, thereby creating and recording in images a personal history. At a deep level, the patient/artist begins to make ties to the world. Just as the process of becoming a parent pulls from one's past and binds one to the future, so too the artist aligns with all that has gone before in the history of art and all that will be in the future as he creates in the present.

Donna's journey in the studio began with a painting of a city street at sunset. The street was empty. Although there were parked cars and OPEN signs on the storefront windows, there were no people. There was a haunting sense of vacancy. I asked her if she had any feeling about the painting. She yawned and said, "No, I'm just glad it's done."

Her second piece was a slightly larger version of the first. Minor details were altered, but the emotional impact of the scene was the same. In an attempt to engage with her about the painting I commented that her style reminded me of the impressionists. She blandly asked, "Who is that?" I had started to explain impressionism when she abruptly stood up, walked to the sink to wash her hands and started a conversation with a boy.

I began to be more hopeful about Donna when one of my colleagues noted that on days when I was not in the studio she would isolate herself in a small side room where she was sure to be left alone with her work. This was in contrast to her usual position in the center of the studio area. Donna's withdrawal seemed to imply some sense of attachment to me and an awareness on her part of her need for structure. When I was there, I provided enough structure that it was safe for her to be in the middle of all the stimulation and commotion of the studio. When I was not there she acknowledged at some level by her isolation that she was unable to structure herself. Among her peers, Donna coined a playful phrase, "paint by Bruce," as opposed to paint by number.

As Donna's journey progressed in the art studio I would occasionally bring in an art history textbook or a book of collected works by one artist. She would leaf through them, sometimes stop to ask a question or comment about what she liked or did not like about a painting. In her own work she developed a style which might best be described as a hybrid of abstract expressionism and minimalism. At first glance her painting would appear chaotic and disorganized. The process she used, however, was highly structured. She began by covering the entire canvas with one solid color. Then she would drip contrasting and complementary colors randomly over the base color. The masking color was repeated. The end product was a multilayered blend of chaos and tight, precise blocks of color and boundary. These paintings took quite some time to complete. My interpretation of her process, which I kept to myself, was that she was making an effort, conscious or not, to structure the inner chaos she felt. In talking about these paintings, Donna said, "I like these. They feel good to me."

At about the same time that Donna was developing this style of painting in the studio, she was referred to the girls' expressive group for which I was co-therapist. There were six adolescent girls in the group. My co-therapist was Lori Brown, R.N. Since all of the girls lived on the same treatment unit, Donna was well known to the other members of the group. Some of the other girls were not happy that Donna would be entering the group. They let Lori and me know that she was in continuous conflict with several of the girls and was not well liked by anyone.

The patients selected for this group tended to be those who were struggling with issues of rage, self-loathing and loneliness. The atmosphere was often blatantly hostile and devaluing. A significant point came for Donna when the graphic task was to draw a time or a place in your life that was safe. Donna covered her page with smudges of black and red. It was very different from the drawings of her peers, which included images of a favorite room at home, or the beach or some place in their hometown. Donna's voice cracked as she shared with the group that there was nowhere that she felt secure. She added that no matter how tough or confident she might appear, she really felt sad and scared all the time.

This was the most open and vulnerable that anyone in the group had ever seen her be. For a few moments she was real and accessible. Later on in the session another patient showed her drawing that depicted her mother's sewing room. Donna commented, "It must be nice to know that you belong."

There are many other vignettes I could offer to illustrate Donna's struggle to create her own sense of history . . . to grow her own roots. She painted a portrait of me as she imagined I must have appeared in the 1960s. She painted a symbolic portrait of her family, how she wished they could be, how they might have been a long time ago, and how they are now. Perhaps the most poignant story of Donna comes from the expressive group. After having completed a drawing on the theme of "life is hard," she drew an analogy from her image to her experience of being in therapy. Her spontaneous interpretation of her own work was, "I know that when I have real feelings I have memories. Memories make me have feelings. It hurts."

Summarizing his view of what it requires to successfully treat ahistorical borderline patients, my colleague, Doctor Robert Huestis, has said, "A personal affective history is necessary for these patients and it must be created. Obviously this implies rather long-term treatment and I do not believe these patients can be treated very effectively in short-term settings." Reflecting on the role of the visual arts in the creation of personal history, Doctor Huestis goes on to say, "These are the windows that the patients allow us to look through as they struggle to create a past so they can function in the future, rather than live only in the present."

Chapter XIII

EXISTENTIAL LEADERSHIP: THE BASIC TASKS

To this point I have considered the underlying suppositions of an existentialist's view of therapy, the arts and illness. In this chapter I will explore the basic tasks of the therapist and reflect on the relative merits of functioning alone as a therapist leader of groups and sharing the tasks with a co-therapist. I wish to reiterate that the consistent positive relationship between patient and therapist underlies all of the efforts and tasks of the therapist. The position of the therapist or co-therapists must be one of concern, acceptance and genuine willingness to engage with the patients in their pain, struggle and risk-taking as they journey to find the meaning of their lives. The therapist must never attempt to enforce his or her own system of belief upon the struggle of the patient. We must always maintain the position that our task is to accompany the patients as they discover for themselves the point of their quest. The most that a therapist or pair of therapists can do is to state verbally, graphically and through their own behavior that the suffering, anguish and insecurities of the patient have value.

Irvin Yalom describes the basic tasks of the therapist in groups to be threefold. The first task is the creation and maintenance of the group. The second is "culture building." As therapist, "You endeavor to establish a code of behavioral rules or norms that will guide the interaction of the group." The third task is to guide the focus of the group to "the here and now."[30]

Applying these three leadership tasks to the expressive art therapy group and individual sessions sheds interesting light on the role of the art therapist. First, I must establish the time and frequency of the sessions. I must provide adequate materials, schedule appropriate studio space. I must close the group when we have reached our maximum and advertise openings when they occur.

As the culture builder, I must shape the mores and expectations of the group, both implicitly and explicitly. For instance, if I want the group to start promptly, I give a powerful implicit message by being punctual and

131

ready to work at the prescribed time. The group or individual patient learns through my example that our time is valuable and deviations are rare.

One expectation is made explicit: confidentiality is important. Patients often quote me as they caution one another, "What you say in here stays in here."

The culture is built and reinforced by my modeling. My investment in the art process, my belief that life has meaning, my punctuality and my openness have tremendous effect on the tone of a session.

The culture expands as the patient assumes a more active role in imparting the history of the group, or explicit rules, etc., to new members. In this way the group maintains its own life. It never ceases to amaze me that contributions made by patients from years ago live on in the group mind. Example: several years ago a tradition of smudging one's cheek was started in a group of adolescent girls. Although the first smudger was discharged years ago, the dirty cheek is still a sign of acceptance of new members. In another group, the tradition is that when a member is discharged, the peer who was closest to him will take over the drawing place of the one who is gone.

Such traditions indicate the establishment of a culture of ownership within the group. While I used to think of them as only of passing interest, I now watch for them and see them as powerful symbols of alliance between individuals and the group. The culture of the expressive art psychotherapy group is strengthened whenever a poignant event of self-disclosure occurs. These are not always recountings of factual events but often are a here-and-now sharing of feelings or associations to the image metaphors. Inevitably at such times, the group members rally to the support and aid of their peer, enhancing the cohesiveness of the group and fostering the sense of safety that is required to face the sufferings and struggles each member brings to the sessions.

Finally, as therapist or co-therapist, I encourage the shaping of the session's culture through consistent adherence to procedural rituals. Every group begins as I close the door and sit down. Every group session consists of a warm-up experience, a primary exercise and a closure process. There are very, very few exceptions to these procedures. The flow of the session becomes engrained as part of the experience of the group. It can be most reassuring to the patient who is caught up for a time in the intensity of his pain, for instance. He knows there will be an opportunity to wind down, to compose himself before he walks out the door. This frees him to experience his feelings more fully.

The third task of the therapist, focusing on the here and now, is of particular importance to the expressive art psychotherapy experience. Based on the belief that all things we create are a self-portrait, the task of the therapist is to empower the patients to own what they have created in the present. In both traditional therapy and group therapy, patients often attempt to distance themselves from their graphics by describing them as representing historic events in their lives that no longer affect them. The power of the art image is that it is a present object, and therapy represents how one feels right now.

An example: Matt, a twenty-five-year-old man, assigned to draw "me and my father," drew a picture of a remote-controlled car. He said he had been given the car for his tenth birthday, but that his father had played with it more than he had. As Matt told the story, he laughed about his dad's playing with the car. When he gave the car image a voice, however, it expressed outrage at being controlled by the father. "I was supposed to be *his* present," the car voice explained angrily. The more we dialogued with the car and later with dad's hands on the remote-control device, the more aware Matt became of his present-day feelings about his domineering father. Without the rubric of keeping content and process in the here and now, the significance of Matt's drawing would have been lost in what seemed at first glance to be a humorous drawing of an old event.

These tasks are multilayered and require intense energy and concentration on the part of the therapist. At the same time the leaders are attending to their tasks, they must also attend to the individual patient and graphic communications within the group. It can be overwhelming work. This brings us to the question of whether to work alone or with a co-therapist in a group. In either case there are advantages and disadvantages that should be carefully considered.

It is perhaps inevitable that we pattern our style after those who trained and taught us the art of healing. I have experienced this from the position of being the apprentice and from the position of mentor/ supervisor. For the student it is nearly impossible to avoid wanting to emulate the master. For the seasoned therapist it is difficult to avoid the narcissistic urge to see your own style reflected in the accomplishments of your student. Just as children incorporate the strengths and weaknesses of their parents into their own personality makeup, so is the apprentice bound to assimilate the assets and deficits of the role model.

The model of leadership that was presented to me in my training was clearly that of an individual primary therapist. The leader's tasks were to maintain the structure of the session, incorporate new members into the group milieu, facilitate the artistic experience and verbal discussion and to maintain the boundaries of the group. In a political sense the leader/therapist was a benevolent dictator.

Don Jones, my mentor, had been leading groups in that way for many years, first at the Menninger Foundation and then at Harding Hospital. The only exceptions to his primary leadership of groups came in the form of concessions to his interns as they (we) made our first faltering attempts at leadership. I recall that at one point in my training Don shared with me a dream he had had the night before. The dream image was of himself riding a horse. He was dressed as Don Quixote. I walked along beside the horse carrying Quixote's lance, clearly in the role of Sancho Panza. This image accurately depicted the roles that Don and I played, not only during the course of my internship, but for years afterward. The model of leadership is clearly one of primary leader. Others were allowed to help along the way, but it was always evident who bore the significant responsibility for leadership.

I replicated this model for years. I preferred to work alone with groups and maintained an autocratic stance when interns were assigned to my groups. The benefits of this singular approach were these:

- Each time I entered the expressive art psychotherapy room I experienced anew the anxiety of being alone. This reminded me of the anguish of my patients. My aloneness helped me to remember how difficult was the work we were about to undertake.

- Being the only therapist in the room forced me to remain intensely focused on the process and content of the images, the individual dynamics and the relationship issues. I had no choice but to be present and attentive.

- By working alone I provided the group with a singular focus for their projected angry, sexual and competitive feelings.

- Being the only leader of the group made it possible for me to have a consistent sense of the direction that the individuals and group were taking.

- Finally, the group members were able to have clear expectations of group procedures for which the therapist was responsible.

There were disadvantages to working alone, as well:

- In moments of intense conflict it was often difficult for me to achieve enough objective distance to observe clearly the phenomenon.
- There is so much information available in the course of an expressive art group, it is overwhelming at times. It is very difficult for one person to attend to all of the imagery, all of the affect, all of the intra- and interpersonal dynamics.
- Disruptions occurred when I was ill or on vacation.
- At times, I found myself immersed in angry or erotic or competitive feelings about my patients. It was very difficult to sort through on my own, even with the aid of supervision.
- Sometimes the feelings of the group were nearly overwhelming and it was most difficult working alone to provide a secure, contained environment for the patient.
- All therapists have blind spots, i.e., issues or concerns that for some reason we are unable to be attuned to. Working alone there was no way to counteract or get beyond my insensitivities.

The pros and cons of individual leadership and co-therapy balance fairly evenly, in my opinion. I have grown suspicious of fervent arguments in favor of one model over another. For many art therapists the concerns are pragmatic rather than philosophical or theoretical: availability of partners, institutional policy. For myself I have grown to enjoy dancing with a partner more than dancing alone. Since my first co-therapy experience with Doctor Carol Lebeiko, I have gone on to form three patient additional groups with co-therapists, as well as one training group for interns. These relationships and the work my co-therapists and I have been able to do with our patients has solidified my investment in shared leadership.

THE RELATIONSHIP VESSEL

The work of maintaining relationships is arduous and never-ending. Ongoing relationships are not finished. Although the work of understanding, supporting, moving away and moving together may plateau for periods of time, it always resumes at some point. The co-therapy relationship is based upon these principles. If it is a good relationship, there is a solid core of understanding and acceptance, but the details and manifestations are continually being negotiated.

The co-therapy relationship forms the vessel or container of the group, whose norms, boundaries, history, mores and feelings are held within it. The container, while being resilient and flexible, also provides enough rigidity to maintain the identity of the group. I suggest that the group will be able to deal in a healthy way with whatever issues of content the co-therapists have made open business in their relationship. If there are areas that the co-therapists have been unwilling to discuss about their relationship, the group will attempt to suppress these issues and will inevitably act them out in pathological ways. There is a complex inter-play of spoken and unspoken feelings and themes. Often, a dynamic system of checks and balances flows beneath the surface between co-therapists and patients.

ILLUSTRATION: Debra DeBrular and I began to work as co-therapists with a group of older adolescent boys. I had been leading the group for six months before her entry. We had often discussed how we felt about the nurturing role she would bring to the group. She is a natural maternal figure who relates in an open and warm way to her patients. Within a few weeks of her initial session, the boys were clearly associating with Deb as the mother of the group. The related affects were positive at times and at other times hostile and caustic. In either case, the themes and feeling emerged quite naturally and were dealt with effectively in the group. Although the patients' feelings about the maternal figure were quite potent and often conflicted, the work we had done in our relationship allowed the group the freedom to express them directly.

In contrast, several months later the boys opened a session with foul and abusive language. They were particularly devaluing of women, whom they described as bitches and cunts. Such language was atypical and without any prior context within the group milieu. I found myself furious at their crudeness and at the same time I became aware of feeling very protective of Deb.

One of the boys suggested that we draw "our wall and then write graffiti on it." The graffiti they covered their walls with was hostile and sexualized. My anger at the group increased.

Deb's wall, however, had a small, frail vine growing upon it. As she spoke of the vine, she said that it was a very feminine vine and it made her aware that she was the only woman in the group. It struck me that Deb and I had spent a lot of time talking about her mother role in the group, yet we had not discussed at all the sexual aspects of her being the only woman. The patients were unconsciously telling us that they could no longer tolerate this absence in Deb's and my relationship. Since that time we have made efforts to discuss the effects of her femininity and my masculinity in our relationship and in the group. There has been no further instance of vulgar acting out since these issues have been made open.

THE DANCE: METAPHORS OF LEADERSHIP

In the fall of 1963, my mother enrolled me in a ballroom dance class. I was in the seventh grade. Over the summer my hormones had exploded and the physical revolution of puberty had begun. I entered the dance class with much excitement, trepidation, hope and fear. The first time I put my arm around my partner's back I was both embarrassed and elated. The first attempts at learning the box-step were awkward. My first stuttering recitation of "May I have this dance?" was clumsy. There were times I longed to run out of the room and never return. I wanted to go back to the days of trading baseball cards or walking alone in the woods, just being a boy. Yet, another part of me kept pulling me back to class every Wednesday night. In time I learned to dance. Life has never been the same, nor would I want it to be.

May I have this dance?

In 1983 John Reece and I presented a paper at Grand Rounds at Harding Hospital on the subject of the use of the arts in the treatment of borderline personality patients. In the audience that morning was Doctor Carol Lebeiko, who had just recently joined the medical staff of the hospital. Following the presentation, Doctor Lebeiko approached us and complimented our work. About a week later she and I were at a luncheon meeting together. She told me she had been thinking a lot about the work I do and was wondering if I might be interested in co-leading an expressive arts psychotherapy group with her. I said it was an interesting idea, a child psychiatrist and an art therapist working together. What I did not say was that I had never had a co-therapist and had never really wanted one. We agreed to meet the following week to discuss the possibilities.

I sat in the cushioned chair in her office and was terribly uncomfortable. She sat at her desk, asking practical questions about when we could hold such a group, how long each session would be, where we might locate it, how much we would charge, etc., etc. As I left her office that morning I wondered what in the world I was getting myself into. I did not like being questioned, I was not sure I wanted to share leadership with anyone and I was clearly uneasy about the power issues inherent in an alliance between a male art therapist and a female psychiatrist. My stomach turned anxiously as I made my way back to my office. In my head I heard the voice of Don Jones saying, "Seek anxiety, Bruce."

Uneasy as I was about this dance, I called Doctor Lebeiko later that day and told her that I was definitely interested in forming a group with her. Although neither Carol nor I spoke of it in these terms, I see now that what I really told her on that afternoon was, "Yes, Carol, I am interested in having a relationship with you." We had accepted each other's invitation to dance.

I am not sure where I first encountered the dance metaphor as a description of co-therapy. I heard it from Cathy Moon as she and Deb Debrular wrote a paper on their co-therapy relationship. Carol Lebeiko used the metaphor early on in one of our post-group discussions. Whoever it was who first used it, I wholeheartedly agree.

Doctor Lebeiko's and my dance has been going on for quite some time now. As I was preparing my notes for this chapter I asked her to talk about her experience of the co-therapy process as it has evolved between us. Here is some of what she said as she spoke of our relationship as co-therapists in an all-female adolescent group:

"Well, there are pragmatic benefits. I don't think the group has ever been canceled, despite vacations or illness of either one of us. There is always a backup. I think early on I had to deal with my dependency issues. Being a woman, I wanted to be sure that you knew that I could run things by myself. There were times that I secretly wished you (Bruce) wouldn't come back from vacation. This really made me look at my control issues. I think we now have a very balanced approach. My medium is words and yours is art. When we put them together it works well for the patients. Plus, you are often able to find something to like and value in patients that I have trouble relating to, and vice versa. For instance, when we drew "things about our bodies that we like or dislike," your being in the group really altered that experience.

"In the times when you are away, I feel a sense of abandonment. There is no one to talk with about the group . . . about what has happened in the group. I know that when we are both in the group I can be more available to the patients. I don't have to be as objective and distant, and I'm more relaxed. I'm freer to dance with individuals in the group.

"Sure, it takes energy to work together. We had to, and have to decide what our dance will be. For me it has to be a mutual relationship, not a master/slave arrangement.

"The other advantage, of course, is that our genders provide for sexual issues to be addressed in the group. They might be looked at if you weren't there with me, but not in the same way.

"Another metaphor to describe co-therapy might be the marriage metaphor. If our relationship is good we'll provide a healthy environment for our patients. If it isn't, we can't. When people discuss the pros and cons of co-therapy they should think of marriage. Some marriages should be annulled, some end in divorce, but some are very good marriages.

"I really agree with you, Bruce, that the co-therapists are the container for the group. Whatever our relationship can tolerate the group will deal with. Whatever our taboos are, the group will avoid. I think now that the cons of co-therapy are so outweighed by positives it's hard to imagine doing the group alone."

This positive view of co-therapy is very different from the conclusions drawn by Rutan and Stone in their work, *Psychodynamic Group Psychotherapy:* "Overall, the disadvantages of co-therapy outweigh the gains that accrue from this leadership format. In training situations there may be some particular advantages to having co-therapy, but a price is paid in the therapist's time and energy, as well as potential complications in the patient's therapy."[31]

As has been the case with my views on all aspects of existential art therapy presented to this point, my ideas on leadership issues have evolved over the years. I now hold a position that I would have opposed a decade ago. Nothing is so consistent in therapy as change.

The choice of a co-therapy partner is an important one, to be made very seriously. As annulments and divorces are painful for married couples, so too the dissolution of co-therapy relationships, on whatever grounds, is painful. It is essential that both parties in the relationship be deeply committed to its success. Time for discussion of plans and reflection on the outcome of sessions is crucial. Partners must be able to speak the same language and to share, at least in large part, the philosophical and theoretical views of each other. At the same time they must be wary of the many temptations that such professional endeavors present. Just as the group members will project their angry, sexual and competitive feelings onto the leaders, the leaders also will inevitably have those same feelings toward each other. It is imperative that both therapists maintain their professional boundaries and focus themselves to the task of putting feelings into images and words, but not actions.

Co-therapy as a model can provide the patient with a relationship devoid of destructive competition, sexual exploitation and aggressive devaluation of the other, which can be tremendously beneficial. Further, it offers a stage on which the drama of engagement with pain, struggle and risk may be played out before the patient's eyes.

Chapter XIV

THE CANVAS MIRROR

Whenever a new student enters the clinical internship in Art Therapy at Harding Hospital, I begin their first didactic seminar on the philosophy of art with the question, "Why do you make art?" Advanced interns invariably turn to one another and smile. They know that the neophyte will be asked this question many times over by the time their training is complete. They also know that I will accept no simple answer, no one-line response, no off-the-top-of-your-head retorts.

For the art therapist in training or the seasoned professional there is no more singularly important question to be asked time and again, "Why do you make art?" It is in the constant searching of our own depths regarding the images we create that the validation of our endeavors with our patients may best be found. I am often perplexed when I hear art therapy colleagues exclaim that they have not painted or drawn for their own sakes in years. As incredible as this may sound, it is often the case that art therapists find themselves too busy or too tired to create art on their own.

My intention in this chapter is to stimulate the reader to examine for himself or herself, "Why do I do art?" It is essential to remain active artistically if we are to stay honest in our profession. The dangers of not doing so are many, but most significant is the damage that artistic inactivity does to the authenticity of the art therapist. To become so immersed in the doing of therapy or the administration of services or the various other demands on your time and energies that you abandon the artistic task itself makes it utterly impossible to be an existential art therapist. It is the art process itself that is the soul of our profession. All of the technical, theoretical or clinical skills one can amass are hollow without an ongoing active involvement with doing art. I suggest that we have no moral or ethical right to ask for or encourage the patient to become involved in the arts if we are unwilling or unable to do the same.

Only artists, Nietzsche said, "dare to show us the human being as he is." We look for the unique and authentic self of our patient that so often has been covered up or masked beyond recognition. This may be at the core of why some art therapists lose track of their own artistic life. Having invested so much energy in attempting to see what is real in others, complete with scars and blemishes, it may seem a frightening task to look into the canvas mirror.

The world has become used to the conventional portraits made by studio photographers. With warm light, filtered lenses and retouching techniques, these studio portraits show, not real people, but glossy visions of how we would wish to be seen. We have grown so accustomed to these inauthentic portraits of self that the possibility of being seen as we are, as we look in the canvas mirror, is threatening.

All art has an existential quality, for its aim is to depict what is real and authentic in life. The aim is to get below the surface, to unmask the hidden depths of things. It is the task of scientists and photographers to provide the world with portraits of what it *looks like.* The artist provides images of what the world *means,* by unveiling the anguish, vitality and turbulent intensity of a given scene and of his or her own essential self.

In the overview to this book I said that there have been times in my life that art has comforted me when I have been in pain, and that it has afflicted me in times I was comfortable. There have been periods of my life when I have looked into the canvas mirror and found images of courage and integrity. I have also seen open wounds, loneliness and cowardice. The dilemma I face as an artist and as an existentialist and certainly as a therapist is that my anguish cannot be hidden or avoided. When I try to run from the canvas's reflection I am intensely aware that I am running, thus intensely aware of what I run from. There is no escape.

I know as I write that all my attempts to convey the depths of art, existentialism and therapy must inevitably reach only the shallows. These are not disciplines for academic inquiry alone. One must *do* art, one must *be* an existentialist and one must *experience* therapy in order to really understand. The best I can do is to share with the reader some of the images from my own mirror. It is not my intent to present these paintings as great works of art. It is my intent to present shards of scattered mirror glass which have torn me, along with polished surfaces that have healed my wounds. If I can do this with integrity, you may be encouraged also to draw or paint, or make songs or dances that will allow you the joy and suffering of seeing yourself as you are, in the canvas mirror.

Some may object to this kind of sharing on my part. It certainly is not the scholarly thing to do. Still, as with all existentialists, I am compelled to write not from an ivory tower but from my experience of life as an artist. I do not view my work as a therapist, educator and supervisor as separate and distinct from my work as an artist. These roles and activities are inextricably blended. To see one is to see them all.

In this I feel a deep sense of responsibility. In every circumstance of my professional and personal life I am aware that I am constantly forced to choose my path carefully, not only for my good, but for the good of others. As an existential art therapist I am continually interacting with artworks and the persons I treat. The whole focus of these encounters is the growth of my patients as I journey with them in their search for meaning in their lives.

As an educator I am again focused on the art of my students as it reflects their development as therapists. The focus here is on the deepening and expansion of the intern's understanding of himself or herself as artist/therapist. The students' artworks invariably reflect their own coming to grips with the anguish they experience both personally and in relationship with patients they treat.

In my role of supervisor within the Adjunctive Therapy department at Harding Hospital, I act as the observing ego for art therapists and non-art therapists alike. My artistic perspective is helpful in this, even with supervisees from other activity disciplines, for I am able to visualize the underlying metaphoric themes they bring to supervision sessions. The focus in these situations is to honor the struggles, sufferings and strengths of those I supervise. I try always to be present and open to them as we meet together to reflect on their experience of themselves as therapists.

Finally, in my own paintings and poems I feel responsibility to the art and to myself, even though I am unencumbered by concern for another. Although I often paint in the company of patients and colleagues, the canvas mirror is a solitary process. Since, as I have said, all art is existential, I cannot stand before a blank canvas without experiencing my ultimate aloneness. It is almost as if the tautness of the stretched surface exists not only as an objective thing but also as an internal subjective feeling. As my brush pushes against the tension of the canvas I feel its pressured touch within me.

A final comment before I turn to discussion of some of the images that have emerged in my work as an artist. Just as I believe that it is imperative that we art therapists engage in ongoing art processes ourselves, I would also propose that it is helpful, perhaps essential, that we also seek out and experience therapy for ourselves. It is terribly important that we understand our own motivations that lead us to the work we do. We must be willing to search ourselves in the same way we ask our patients to. Surely this is a painful and frightening task, but it can bring a deeper sense of understanding and fullness, not only to our work, but to our whole selves as well. All too often we therapists regard ourselves as being nearly superhuman and "having it all together." To acknowledge and own our vulnerabilities, fears and pains can do no more than deepen our commitment to the difficult work that we and our patients engage in daily. The reality is that no one seeks therapy when life is satisfying and meaningful. I encourage the reader not to be shy about seeking help for yourself when life presents you with its irreparable losses and difficulties, as it surely will at some point.

IMAGES FROM THE MIRROR

The paintings that follow were created over a period of ten years. In each of them there are recurring images. Representations of a wheat field, for instance, occur in various forms. Sometimes the field is a prominent element in the painting. At other times it is a minor fragment of background. These field images interest me, for they were not included in the paintings with conscious intent. It was not until my therapist, Doctor Jim Lantz, asked me to bring retrospective photographs of my work that I was even aware of this recurring theme. Jim Lantz is a diplomate in logotherapy and was most interested in the meanings that I expressed on canvas.

In my work, whether poetry or painting, I like to juxtapose images that have meaning for me. I often arrange them in ways that are realistically impossible but symbolically significant in my inner world.

The first painting (Fig. 5) is both interior and exterior. The window is the passageway between those two different worlds. I see myself as both an onlooker inside the room and as the naked man standing in the field. In my position in the room I am warm but feel a draft coming from the slightly opened door. As the man in the field I feel a stiff breeze that whips the green cloth I hold on my right arm. There are several interesting details in this piece, but its overall emotional tone for me is a vague sense of loneliness and conflict. This painting was done three or four years after I had been forced to withdraw as a clergyman from the

Methodist Church. It was the view of the authorities in the church organization that special ministries such as mine were to be discouraged. At that time they did all they could to direct clergy away from pursuing counseling ministries and all other non-parish pursuits.

Figure 5. *Opening Wind.*

My initial emotional response to the Methodist hierarchy was to be angry and withdrawn. This painting, however, put me in touch with the sense of abandonment and disappointment I felt. The wine bottle representing the sacraments and the apple symbolize the nourishment that having once been an "insider" had brought. The naked man in the field is vulnerable to the elements outside the warmth of the room and terribly distant from the church on the horizon.

As a therapist I am always looking out for dualities in my patients. This painting reminded me of the poles within myself. In working with patients and in being attuned to myself I am aware that wherever anger is portrayed, hurt lurks in the shadows; that whenever happiness and contentment are depicted, sadness and turmoil are close by.

The second painting, *Homage to the Game,* was originally intended as a tongue-in-cheek spoof on my interest in basketball (Fig. 6). I meant to be playful and perhaps a little silly. The image that took over as I painted, however, is anything but a joke to me. Cast in surreal lighting, an arm rises out of the earth, about to receive a pass. The more I worked on this image, the more disturbing it became for me. Again, the wheat field is in the background, this time reflecting the eerie glow from a light source we cannot see. It is bordered by a deep blue body of water. As I imagine myself standing by this pool, it seems very cool, clear and bottomless. Having completed the background elements, I used the bottom of a wastebasket to trace the outline of the basketball.

When I finished the painting I felt miserable about it. It was not playful at all, and I quickly stored it away in the garage. I did not know exactly why I disliked it so much and I clearly did not want to look at it. A few years later the significance of my having thoughtlessly using a trash can to make the outline became more apparent. The game of basketball has so many associations for me. I remember my mother hanging a wooden basket on our basement door when I was seven years old. There is no way to estimate how many hours I spent dribbling and shooting baskets in that basement, all the while imagining myself as a college player someday.

Basketball represents years of hard work, fun and friendships from the fifth grade until I was a sophomore in high school. That year I crushed my heel and was prevented from participating in any sport until I was a senior. I was cut from the team that year. I had simply lost too much ground to other players by not being able to compete for two years.

Basketball symbolizes night out with the guys as we got together after work on Wednesday evenings in winter and played pickup games for an hour or so, then went to someone's house to watch the Game of the Week on television.

Finally and maybe most disturbingly, basketball represents my experience with this aging body of mine. Everytime I play I am reminded that I can no longer do the things I did at 25, much less 18. I am two steps slower, I tire faster and, oh, how I ache the next day.

So it is that this painting that was intended as a playful, visual joke on myself stirs deep feelings of joy, camaraderie, failure and the unavoidable realities of my own mortality. Some joke!

As a therapist I have been sensitized to such issues as my adolescent patients flaunt their naive belief in their omnipotent indestructibility, and as I feel the embarrassed frustration of an impotent 50-year-old school teacher. Anguish, my own and others, presents itself in polar extremes and intense bursts of awareness of the way life is.

The art forms that I most often use are painting, poetry and song writing. On occasion these inform one another, complement and immerse

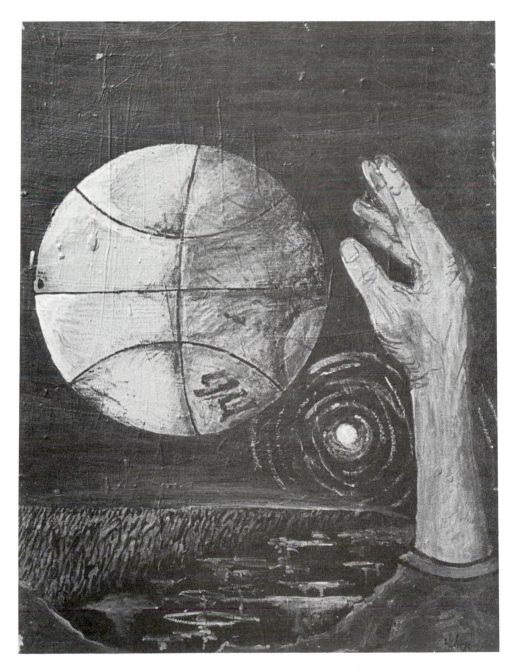

Figure 6. *Basketball:* "Cast in surreal lighting an arm rises out of the earth about to receive a pass."

interdependently. This third painting is one such example. It came as an illustration of a poem-song I wrote titled *Is Anybody Free?* I will let the words and images speak for themselves:

There was a woman, she went out sailing
looking for a home
Adrift upon a river, sailing all alone
And she says, if I only had an anchor
or a port I could crawl into
But she says it so damned wryly
I wonder if it's true
'cause she laughed when I talked of farming
or living up in the woods
Shakes her head in a quiet way
and says, Me I never could
then she sets her sail for somewhere
she's never been before
All she really wants is freedom
she'll be sailing for evermore

I have a friend out in the desert
all he wants is just one drink
but the sand and the sun and he's hoping
it makes him stop and think
and he says, if I only had a bottle of rum
or maybe just one glass of beer
I wouldn't mind all this walking
I could stand the heat out here
but he knows there is no oasis
within the life he leads
he shakes his head in a tired way
and plants his cactus seeds
then he spies one more desert mirage
and walks out one time more
just one little taste of freedom
but he'll be thirsty evermore

And myself, I work in the asylum
a keeper of some keys
and I talk with all my sad people there
I listen to their pleas
I say it's alright, it's alright my friends
who can say who's better off
there are tricky currents on the river
and the desert gets pretty rough
and cities aren't what they used to be

nobody knows what it's about
and the only difference between you and me
is you're inside and I'm out
but later when I'm all alone
sometimes I start to bleed
I ask myself this question
Is anybody really free?
Is anybody really free?

Figure 7. *History:* "A Keeper of some keys."

In the painting, *The Real Thing,* the wheat field is divided by a dirt road (Fig. 8). A man is running active sprints toward the viewer. To one side we catch a glimpse of a Coke billboard, and nearby a window through which we see an ocean at sunset. Above, the sky is clouded and ominous. In the extreme foreground there is the remnant of a shattered stained-glass window. The image holds a sense of desperation for me. The man is not out for a pleasant afternoon jog through the country; he is running from something.

Figure 8. *The Real Thing* " my life was filled with hushed whispers of doubt.."

I painted this piece during a period of my life that was filled with hushed whispers of doubt which nagged me at the deepest of levels. I did not want to listen to these voices who questioned the foundations of my life. Whenever I slowed down long enough I wondered about my competence as a father, my adequacy as a lover and husband and my skill as a therapist. I ran from these questions, both figuratively and literally.

In the figurative sense I kept myself overly busy by working long hours at the hospital, teaching two nights a week at the Columbus College of Art and Design and engaging in miscellaneous other projects that served to keep my pace sufficiently hectic to avoid introspection.

In the literal sense, I became addicted to long-distance running. I built my physical tolerance to the point that five- and ten-mile rounds were comfortable. I ran and ran and ran.

The painting intensifies my awareness of my flight. Gradually, I recognized what I was running from. Not long after this piece was completed, the emotional clouds rolled in and the storm arrived. Through the physical act of running, building my endurance and stretching my potential I learned to face the pain of shortness of breath, fatigue and blistered soles. I learned to keep going, to run through the pain. This painting and others from that period taught me to face the emotional turmoil of my existence. All long-distance runners learn to embrace "the wall" that inevitably confronts them at some point on their trek. As a therapist I believe that engaging in artistic tasks is a potent healing process that empowers the patient/artist to embrace the suffering of the situation and detect its meaning.

The last painting I want to discuss is one of those very rare images that simply walks up and presents itself in its entirety, as if to say, "Here I am, paint me" (Fig. 9). The images came as I was stretching the canvas. They spoke in a gentle, reassuring voice. Unlike many of the images I create, these hold a feeling of warmth, softness and connectedness for me. No ominous clouds or vast lonely places are present. There is a feeling of intangible warmth and intimacy. Keys hang upon the wall awaiting use. The apple is ripe, ready to be eaten. The candle is lit as if for a romantic quiet evening. A gift of flowers has been made and a frayed rope has been rebraided. There are hints of the other pole, however. There are shadows cast by the light, and a few rose petals and leaves lie on the tablecloth. Still, the message of this painting, which all but painted itself, is *the wounds are healed.* As I signed it, I felt a wave of elation wash over me. If I had to give it a title I would call this painting *Yes.*

Figure 9. *Precious Gifts:* " one of those very rare images which simply walks up and presents itself in its entirety, as if to say, 'Here I am, paint me.'"

In my work with patients I am never more in awe of the power of the arts than when I see them back away from their work, quietly nod their heads and then just look at what they have done. I often wish their drawings and sculptures would really speak and that I could listen to the conversations between the soul of the artist and the fruits of its labor. But that is a private dialogue, far below the hearing range of others. Even if such things could be heard, I doubt they could be understood.

These five paintings represent a cross section of the art I create. They have been my affliction and my comfort. They have pushed and jabbed me and they have held me tenderly. They have at times demanded that I open my eyes and look at the monstrous pain; they have brought honor to my suffering. The images I make have soothed the emptiness left by the losses I have encountered.

Amid their turbulence I have felt the breath of peace. During their moans of despair I have heard their melodies of hope. This is why I make art.

Why do you make art?
Why do you make art?
Why do you make art?

As for the rest of these paintings, you decide what their stories are (Figs. 10–21). Better yet, go paint your own.

Figure 10. *Foundations and Time.*

Figure 11. *Strawberries.*

Figure 12. *Covering.*

Figure 13. *A Bitterness.*

Figure 14. *Someplace Deep.*

Figure 15. *Post.*

Figure 16. *Picnic in Memory.*

Figure 17. *Waiting.*

Figure 18. *Communion.*

Figure 19. *Morning Coffee.*

Figure 20. *A Passing Blindness.*

Figure 21. *Stage Racing.*

AFTERWORD

Our journey is nearly complete. We have traveled from existentialist beginning points through chaos and emptiness toward meaning and fullness. Along the way I have offered hints at a methodology, but mostly I have refrained from saying too much about how to do anything. I have tried to present a way of thinking and of looking at things. I have written a fair amount on the nature of creative activity and I have spun some metaphoric tales. I hope you got the point. In addition, I have provided the reader with some provocative reflections on the role society and culture play in fostering illness ... or maybe it is the other way around. I believe I have revisited the deep roots of our profession. It is my most sincere wish that these roots will stand out in sharp contrast to those who would steer us and future generations of art therapists toward scientific research, quantifiable data and measurable outcome surveys, and away from soul, spirit and image.

I must qualify that statement. I am not opposed to research activities, but I do proclaim as loudly as possible, "WHAT WE ART THERAPISTS DO CANNOT BE MEASURED OR COUNTED!"

Finally, I took a risk by including several of my own paintings and a discussion of them. This was risky at several levels. What if you look at my paintings and decide that I am overindulging my narcissism? What if you look at my paintings and say to yourself, "What garbage is this?" Or, what if you look at them and see blemishes or scars that even I did not know existed? None of these prospects is comfortable to me. But then, existentialism, art and therapy are all about risk-taking and I hope you understand.

Peace,

Bruce L. Moon

BIBLIOGRAPHY

1. McLean, Don. "American Pie" (LP). New York: United Artists Records, 1971.
2. McNiff, Shawn. *The Arts and Psychotherapy.* Springfield, IL: Charles C Thomas. Publisher, 1983.
3. Simon, Paul. "Hearts and Bones" (LP). New York: Warner Brothers Records, 1983.
4. Kopp, Sheldon. *If You Meet the Buddha on the Road, Kill Him.* Palo Alto, CA: Science and Behavior Books, 1972.
5. Rinsley, Donald. *Treatment of the Severely Disturbed Adolescent.* New York: Jason Aronson, 1983.
6. Bach, Richard. *Jonathan Livingston Seagull.* New York: MacMillan, 1970.
7. Kafka, Franz. *The Castle.* New York, Modern Library, 1954, 1969.
8. The Beatles; Harrison, George. "I, Me, Mine" (Let It Be LP). New York: Apple Records, 1970.
9. Frankl, Viktor. *Man's Search for Meaning: An Introduction to Logotherapy.* Washington Square Press, 1953, 1969.
10. Rolling Stones. "You Can't Always Get What You Want" (Let It Bleed LP; New York, ABKCO Records 1986). London: London Records, 1971.
11. Heinlein, Robert A. *A Stranger in a Strange Land.* New York, Putnam, 1961.
12. King, Stephen. *Misery.* New York: Penguin, 1988.
13. Crosson, John Dominic. *In Parables.* New York: Harper and Row, 1973.
14. Jensen, Richard A. *Telling the Story.* Minneapolis, Augsburg, 1980.
15. McNiff, Shawn. *Fundamentals of Art Therapy.* Springfield, IL: Charles C Thomas. Publisher, 1988.
16. Hoffer, Eric. *The True Believer.* New York: Harper and Row, 1951.
17. Dylan, Bob. *Writings and Drawings of Bob Dylan.* New York: Alfred A. Knopf, 1973.
18. Jaffe, Aniela. In C. G. Jung, *Man and His Symbols.* New York: J. G. Ferguson, 1964.
19. Janson, H. W. *History of Art.* New York: Harry N. Abrams, 1971.
20. Frankl, Viktor. *The Doctor and the Soul.* New York: Alfred A. Knopf, 1955.
21. Peck, M. Scott. *The Road Less Traveled.* New York: Simon and Schuster, 1978.
22. Vonnegut, Kurt. *Bluebeard.* New York: Delacorte Press, 1982.
23. *Webster's New Collegiate Dictionary.* Springfield, MA: G. & C. Merrian Company, 1956.
24. Mitchell, Joni. "Real Good For Free." Los Angeles: Asylum Records, 1974.
25. Jones G. William. *The Innovator.* Nashville: Abingdon Press, 1962.

26. Fromm, Eric. *The Sane Society.* New York: Fawcett World Library, 1955.
27. Sting. "Russians" (The Dream of the Blue Turtles LP). Los Angeles: A. M. Records, 1987.
28. Simon, Paul. "I Am A Rock" (Sounds of Silence LP). New York, Eclectic Music, Columbia, 1965.
29. Vonnegut, Kurt. *Deadeye Dick.* New York, Delacorte Press, 1982.
30. Yalom, Irvin D. *Theory and Practice of Group Psychotherapy.* New York: Basic Books, 1975.
31. Rutan, J. Scott and Stone, Walter N. *Psychodynamic Group Psychotherapy.* New York: MacMillan, 1984.

INDEX